Dear Hilary,

        thank you for your support and loving friendship.

    Much love,

        Jai

The Keys To The Kingdom

Jai Wurfbain

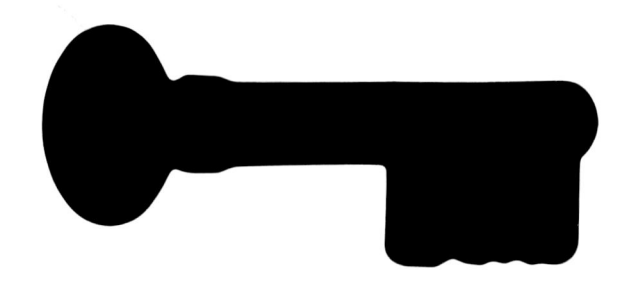

The Keys to the Kingdom

HOPE

Jai Wurfbain

The Kingdom Key Publishing

Published by The Kingdom Key Publishing
17413 Port Marnock Dr.
San Diego, CA 92064
www.thekingdomkey.com

The Keys to the Kingdom – HOPE
ISBN 978-0-692-85966-7

Copyright © 2017 by Jai Wurfbain

All rights reserved. This book or any portion thereof may not be reproduced or used in any manner whatsoever without the express written permission of the writer except for the use of brief quotations in a book review.

Cover design by Chris Buchanan.

Edited by Chet Turnbeaugh

Graphic Production by Daria Lacy

Key and book, manufactured in China.

Published April 1, 2017.

First Printing April, 2017.

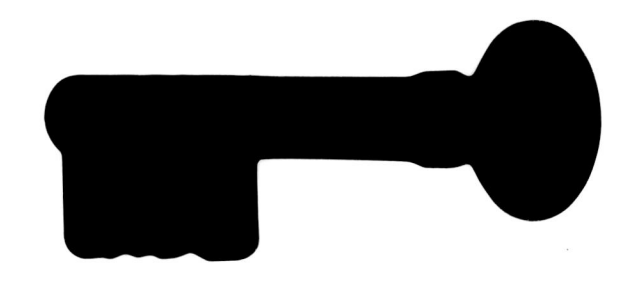

Acknowledgements

Writing this book was not easy. It has been an exhilarating process, but very draining in an emotional and spiritual sense.

I was helped in very significant ways as I was writing this book on HOPE, and I want to extend sincere gratitude to those individuals who were there for me urging me to continue and push on, as well as a myriad of people who pored over my words, chapters, and issues that I was writing about almost as much as I did. This book could not have been written without them.

Special thanks to my loving friend Tom, who has been there through thick and thin. Opening his home for me and giving me sanctuary, physically as well as emotionally.

Thanks to Jim, Gloria and Anja and for adding immeasurably to the editing process of this project as well as your loving friendship.

Also, a special mention to those close friends, who kept my world together. Thank you, Perry, Troy, Christine, Dave, Martha, Brad, Jos, Tricky-Dicky and Vikki.

My editor Chet Turnbeaugh and my graphic design genius MrChrisby.

Daria Lacy for the interior pre-print production.

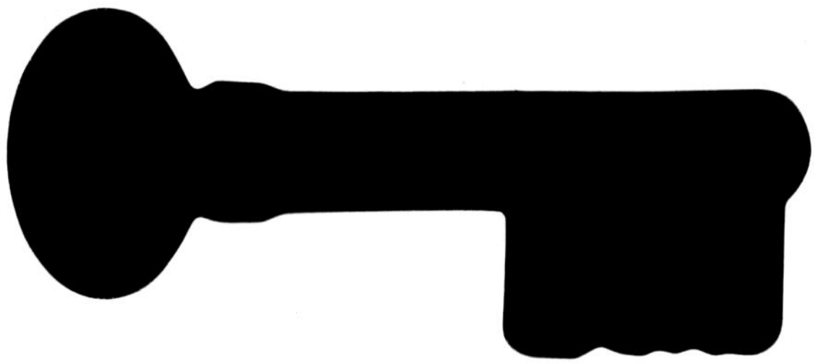

INTRODUCTION

HOPE may be of help to anyone struggling with seemingly insurmountable challenges in life. If you ever had to bounce back from a failed relationship, recoup any kind of loss, convalesce from an illness, or just recover from a bad day, then this book will be beneficial.

This is my story, the story of a young man who literally rode to the top of his financial world on a crest of ego and alcohol, who crashed badly, and who nevertheless rose from the ashes with the help of certain spiritual concepts. I was able to move from "hopelessness" to "faith" by becoming aware of the ignorant beliefs that had unknowingly kept me blind to the abundance I already had in my life.

In other subsequent books in this series, I will share the stories of others who found that acceptance of these keys helped them to sort out their lives and to live in peace as well.

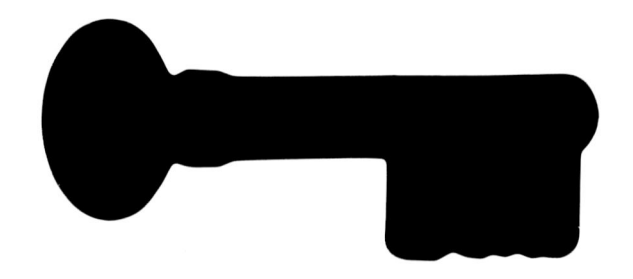

Perhaps these keys can help you or someone you love. This is my hope.

Other books in the series;

- Love
- Faith
- Joy
- Open
- Home
- Gratitude
- Us

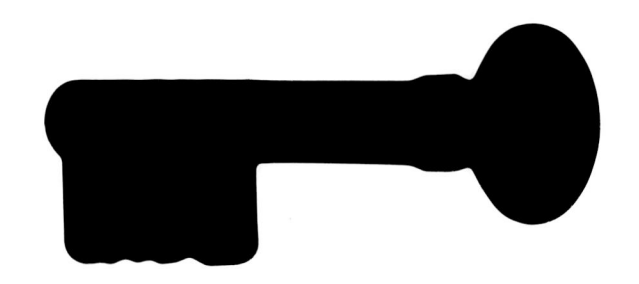

Contents

Acknowledgements ... iii
INTRODUCTION ... v
The Broken Mirror: My Broken Life ... 1
A New Life ... 7
Growing Up ... 10
Climbing The Ladder ... 20
The First Crash ... 25
A False Dawn ... 34
New Depths ... 47
Removing The Blinders ... 56
Loneliness ... 66
Permanence ... 75
Powerlessness ... 85
A Second Wind ... 95
The Golden Rule ... 108
Epilogue ... 118
Kickstarter sponsorship ... 122
Disclaimer ... 123

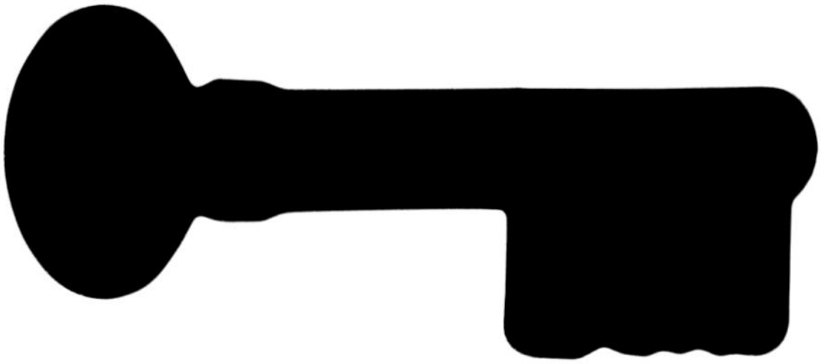

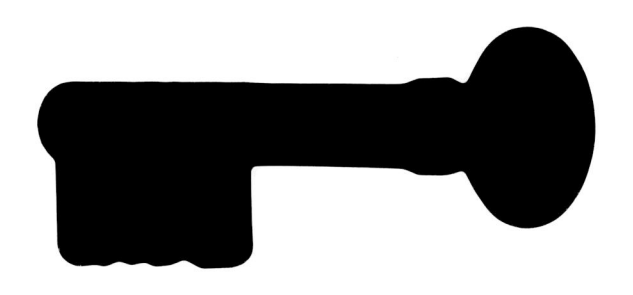

THE BROKEN MIRROR: MY BROKEN LIFE

There was a long moment of silence as I rolled over to check the alarm clock. *Why was my head hurting so bad? Where had I been last night?* I was feeling the craziness of yesterday's binge resurface in my mind. As I struggled to understand how I'd overslept, I began remembering something. But what was it? An argument? A missed business dinner? Something.

I rubbed my eyes and looked for my glasses to check the time. The red blink of the alarm clock was signaling a fear of dread in the back of my mind. I was late and I knew it. The red dots confirmed that I would need to call in sick, or try to come up with a great excuse.

Jai Wurfbain

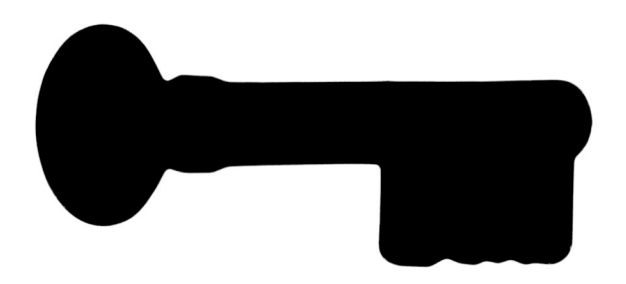

My side of the bedroom was a mess. My shirt from yesterday was crumpled, with trousers, neckties, and underwear littered on the floor. I fumbled around for a moment or two before recognizing that I was alone. Without knowing it, I had misplaced my wallet, my car keys, my cell phone, and oddly enough, my wife.

It was strange that she hadn't woken me. I called out for her in the darkness. Silence answered back. The stillness was thick in the room, as I tried to put the pieces of this broken puzzle back together. I woke up feeling guilty of something. Like I had committed some crime that I could no longer remember. My brain was awash with the toxicity of my hangover. And every thought of self-loathing was crowded out by my drunken stupor. I could see the faint glow of a mirror in the back of my mind. It was just a flashing image and it shattered into a million pieces. It was gone, almost as quickly as it had appeared, as I opened my eyes.

This wasn't the first time I'd woken up with a foggy mind. My drinking was out of control. But I couldn't really come to admit that. I knew that in the back of my mind, something needed to change, but I wasn't going to start believing that quite yet. My love for drink had been consistent since my first few pints as a

The Broken Mirror: My Broken Life

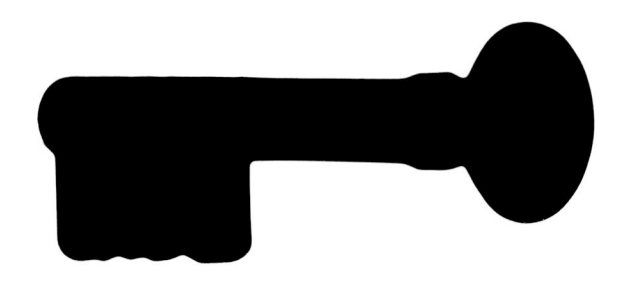

troubled teenager. My lust for anything that would take me out of my mind was immense.

I picked up my shoes. They were designer, and cost more than a month of rent for most of the world's population. Money and power were the two ideals into which, I placed my faith and my trust. And I loved to show them off any chance I got. On the outside I was everything we were taught to be. I was successful; I had a dream job, a dream wife, and was doing everything perfectly. Except that my life was falling apart. I was drinking erratically, walking to pubs at lunch and stumbling out in the evenings. I had kicked a brief cocaine habit, and was struggling in my marriage. I was selfish, and the most conceited individual that I knew. My posh demeanor covered up my inner insecurities. Behind it all, I was afraid.

When I finally pulled on some pants and a shirt, the clock read ten minutes to 7am. I was more than late--I was *MIA*. I picked up my shoes and waltzed into the kitchen, expecting my wife to make me a nice cup of tea. But when I heard the sink running, I knew that something was wrong.

I will chronicle the details of what transpired that morning later on in this book. But this was my moment, where everything shattered. My life crashed around me like little waves in the ocean rippling out to a much larger problem in the depths of my soul. My mind was a mess as it reared to pick up all the broken pieces, but it was no use--the damage was already done.

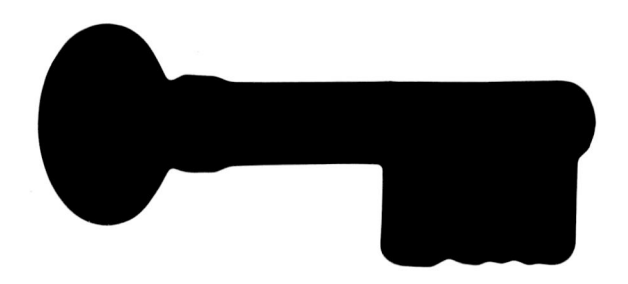

When my wife told me that I had threatened to hurt her after a drunken binge I nearly fainted. She went on to tell me that the police had to come to insure her safety. This was the moment where I lost hope--where everything broke down and fell apart. My life as I knew it was completely over, and I would have to finally face my own actions.

We've all gone through trauma in our lives. We've been hurt by others, we've hurt them, and at some point we've even hurt ourselves. We've fallen down at times into periods of self-despair. We've set markers for ourselves, and we've fallen short of them. This is the story of hope.

Most people would like to believe that we must be optimistic all of the time. They have this misguided notion that we need to put on false personas of happiness, and that we can't allow sadness or fear. This simply isn't true. Gaining and maintaining hope in your life is about having so much more. Having hope is about finding the thin line between utter despair and believing that some day things can change. This book is going to show you that no matter what kind of struggle you are facing you can overcome the depths of sadness, loneliness, and inner turmoil in order to become a bigger, braver you! It will give you the path to wellbeing and set you free from the limitations of who you *were*. Your greatest moments in life lie ahead after reading this book. And while this isn't meant to be prescriptive of every problem in life, I encourage you to use this book as a guide. You've been granted the keys to the kingdom. Know that you have an abundance of hope, and so much well being right beneath your fingertips!

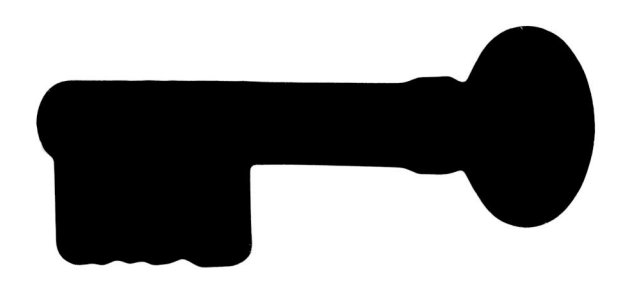

This book is inspired and borne out of love. Love for mankind, love for myself, and love for the idea and concept of a Higher Power. If we are to truly live out lives of success we must believe in the Hope that exists for each one of us. And it is my strongest desire that you will find hope within the pages of this book and cherish *Hope's* truth for all the days of your life.

When we share our story and are vulnerable, we are met with courage. For it takes courage to face ourselves. In this way, I have showed you some of my biggest challenges, the spaces where I am shallow and the areas where I still have yet to grow. It is my sincere believe that my suffering was necessary for me to be open to its lessons, but people with wisdom don't have to learn through their own mistakes. They can do so through the mistakes of others. And to make sure of this, I've written my story at length to serve as a guide for the universal feeling of hopelessness and loneliness. These struggles can be overcome, and you can become the person you want to be.

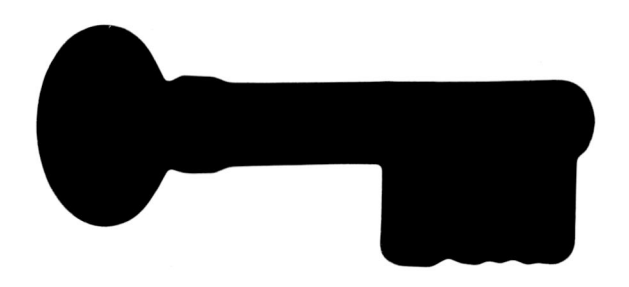

This book is your key to the infinite hope that lies within you. When you believe this to the depth of your being, you will begin to see that the Kingdom is much greater than your pain, your suffering, or your despair. The Kingdom, and incidentally the Key of Hope, are for you to open doorways to something much greater in your life, and to give you access to a higher future version of yourself.

With much love and gratitude I pen these words to you. As you read this book, know that times may be hard, but there is always a greater sunrise not so far away!

A NEW LIFE

I was born in 1970. It says so on my Korean birth certificate. It also reads that I was born in Seoul, South Korea. Other than this information, I only know a few things about my confirmed life in my native land of Korea. Everything else are partial dreams, fear and speculation.

At a very early age, two lovely parents from the Netherlands adopted one of my biological sisters and I. At the time, I was only three years old and my sister, Hélène, was only eighteen months older. My adoption papers reveal that my biological father died suddenly, despite being in otherwise good health. The papers also suggest that we have several more brothers and sisters, all older than us, but whom I've never met. I'm told that I was very sick when my sister and I were given up for adoption. Apparently, we were adopted together because we were the youngest. Without a working father it became necessary for our biological mother to bring in more money.

Jai Wurfbain

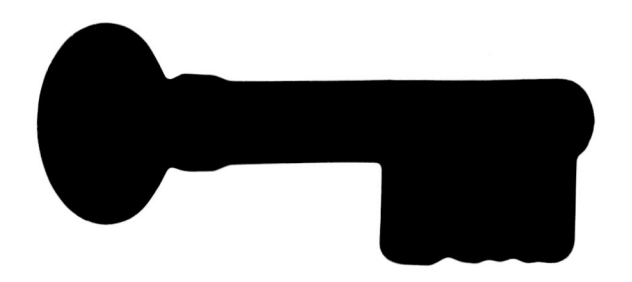

I remember nothing of my time in Korea with certainty. I have some vague, foggy images such as walking miles up a mountain road carrying something. My memory is very sparse, save for a few fuzzy snapshot images of the inside of a dirty, old shed. Hélène has confirmed that these are also her memories, but I cannot reconcile them to be true due to our age at the time. She has always been reluctant to talk to me about them. It's obvious to me that she must suffer some of the same early memories, because she once told me that we were abused. Luckily, I have no recollection of this. I have never actually felt the need to know concrete facts about my early childhood, since I never felt a connection with Korea growing up. When the time is right, maybe she will let me in on her memories, and maybe some of mine will become clearer.

Hélène and I landed at Schiphol Airport, Amsterdam in late August of 1973. We had flown in a Boeing 747, which was filled with young Korean children that had been adopted by European couples eager to start a family. Somewhere in a box with memorabilia, there is a small metal die-cast model of the plane with its blue KLM livery that I was given at that time. My parents will

A New Life

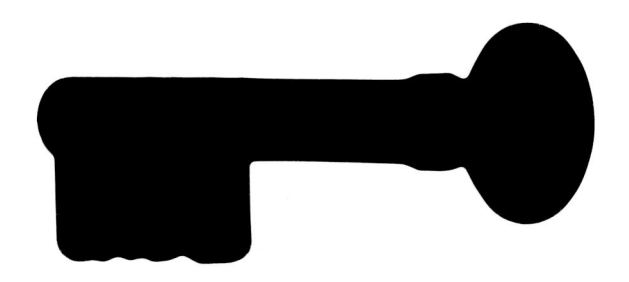

never forget how tightly I held that plane in my little fist when they first saw us.

During that time, it was very popular for European and American families to adopt children from South Korea due to the Korean War. Almost one million children were placed with new families, worldwide. The aftermath of the war left a great vacuum for children whose parents had died fighting, or who were trapped by the tremendous poverty created by the civil war. Hélène celebrated her birthday just three days before we flew out of Korea. I wish I knew how she felt that day. Ironically, we arrived in Holland on our new mother's birthday, which made it a very exciting week for our new family unit, and helped us to glue as a family.

We were picked up at the airport by our new parents and grandparents. I don't remember anything about this except for my grandfather's car, which just seemed to be unbelievably regal and luxurious. It was a brand-new Citroen DS (a highly desirable French classic today,) and I was in complete awe when I saw it. My grandfather used to remind me how utterly amazed I was when they picked us up, my face beaming with astonishment and admiration.

GROWING UP

We were quick to learn the Dutch language as we settled into our new life. Thankfully, we found out that hunger no longer appeared to be a concern. Our new parents had been advised to learn several phrases in Korean, such as: "don't bite," "don't kick," "you can eat that," and "everything is ok." Can you imagine the emotions that everyone must have been going through? My sister and I were also regular visitors at the doctor's office early on, since we were completely unaccustomed to western bacteria and fungi. We even brought over some of our own Korean specimens. Both of us were treated for ringworm, and other *lovely* illnesses.

Johan and Ineke, our new parents, were by no means wealthy, but they made ends meet for us. They provided us with a normal childhood where we could enjoy the benefit of growing up without troubles. My father had been a sea captain in the Merchant Navy for most of his work career, transporting global freight. He had also carried the financial weight of the family. He worked silently, without protest. He was undoubtedly a workaholic. I always felt a little bad for my father, because upon my mother's insistence, he found a new job before we came along. Being home more meant that he could be active in our lives, which is something that to this day, I am still very grateful for. Mom was a "stay-at-home" mom, which allowed us to get the best care possible.

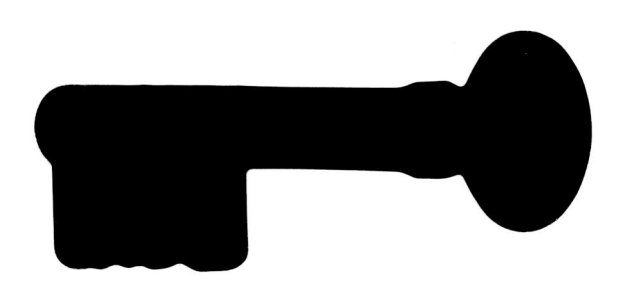

I have fun memories of playing with neighborhood children while roaming freely about in the village and the surrounding countryside. There was, at that time, very little fear for parents to keep children within earshot. We acted as autonomous groups and we moved around in little gangs, simply having fun outside. The only negativity that I remember was the fact that my sister and I were the only kids who weren't blonde, blue-eyed and tall. This often led to me fighting with some of the other children when they belittled us for being "different." I have since learned that this is a trope of children everywhere. But looking back, it felt like I was constantly fighting against some sort of prejudice and injustice daily.

When I was twelve years old, a year after having started middle school, my father accepted a job in London. It was decided that the whole family would immigrate to England. This was not happy news for me, and I was very upset to leave all my friends behind. My unhappiness grew even stronger on my first day at my new school. I spoke very little English, and the whole class erupted in laughter when I was introduced to the class. I had no clue, why they did that, but it certainly hurt my feelings. Later that week, I fought with one boy, Nicholas, who was the biggest, loudest and most obnoxious kid in my class. We eventually became and still remain, the best of friends.

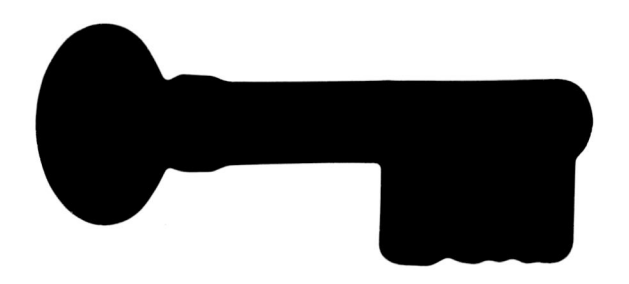

It was only once I joined a Judo club in the evenings that I began to feel a little more comfortable with my new environment. I had practiced judo since I was four years old. I was very good on the mat and pretty quickly became known as a martial arts expert within my local community. This gave me a renewed sense of power, which won me more respect with the other children. As a thirteen-year old boy, I was teaching adults, and children alike, all the physical aspects of Judo. I also began enjoying some real success, myself, in competitions.

I began improving and I fondly remember being drafted to the

Growing Up

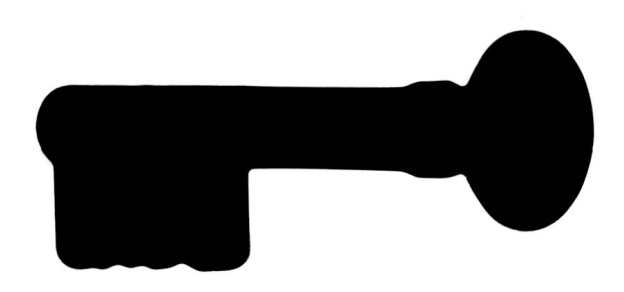

junior national camps, where I was honoured to fight for England in international competitions. I began to better my understanding of the English language. As my knowledge of words grew, so did my confidence. My school was renowned for its rugby team, and I soon found that my natural drive and aggression were very useful on the rugby pitch. I became an integral member of the rugby team and I added a pillar of strength to our already strong frontline. I had learned that I could frighten the opposition by shrugging off physical pain with an evil grin.

Life is about being able to "take the hits and keep going," as the fictitious fighter, Rocky Balboa, would say. I've learned that the most successful people don't see their fear, their pain, or their setbacks as obstacles, but rather as opportunities to use to their advantage. As a martial artist, rugby player, and even later in life as a corporate financier, I needed to be able to get punched in the face and keep moving. It was absolutely essential to my willingness to play the game of life. Ever since I was a small boy, I have been determined to win.

Our rugby coach was a tough Welshman, who had been a keen player himself. I'll never forget the phrase he used to motivate us before every game, *"Get your retaliation in first, laddies!"* It was even funnier because of his thick, Welsh accent. This approach was something that I took as a life-strategy, and still use today in many respects. Although I prided myself on my abilities as an athlete, I was at best only a very average student. I was also quite possibly the laziest one. I just didn't feel the need to do well with my grades, and I was perfectly happy with a passing mark, whether it was fifty-one-percent or one-hundred-percent. Both, meant the same thing to me: *I passed.*

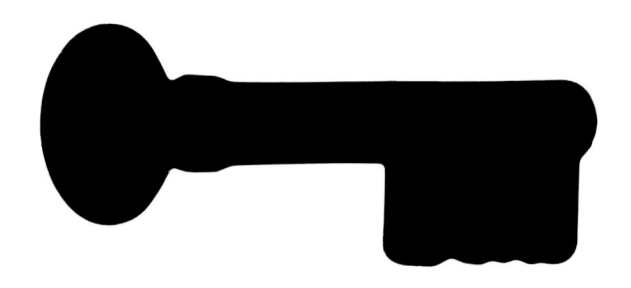

I did come to figure out, however, that if I didn't have to do any work to pass, then I could devote that extra time to do what I wanted to do. Looking back, in my studies, I went to such great lengths to avoid doing work or hiding the fact that I wasn't doing any, that I may as well have done it and have saved myself the time and stress of getting caught.

I started to work the weekends at a restaurant nearby, which was owned and managed by the parents of a school friend. I worked hard, and my supervisors were always pleased by the diligence and attitude that I displayed at work. I was willing, adaptable, hard working and very charming to everyone around me. They gave me small pay raises and moved me from dishwashing to food prepping, bussing, and even bar tending when things got really busy! I looked a lot older than fifteen. The staff loved having my cheerful, happy demeanor around, and being accepted by my peers made me feel good about myself. The paychecks each week were incredible for a child of fifteen, and the most pleasing thing was that no one could tell me how to spend my money or what to spend it on. Money in my pocket gave me a tremendous sense of power. I had more money than anyone else my age, which of course further increased my feelings of self-worth and confidence in myself. But then, one day, during the middle of my high school exams, dark clouds signaling the coming storm gathered.

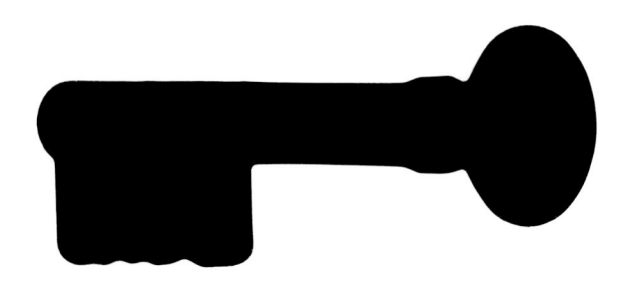

For some reason, my friends and I decided to walk some twenty minutes from the school to a local "pub" and have a drink. None of us had ever been to a pub before without our parents, and I don't know who brought up the idea, especially since it was noon during exams. It might have even been me. For the life of me, I don't know what made us believe that it was a smart idea. Regardless of our thought processes, there were about eight of us that sat down for an extended lunch that day. "The Woolpack," was a quiet pub that was a little out of the way and generally pretty deserted. The owner must have been pleased as punch to have a group of snot-nosed kids burst in pretending to be of drinking age, despite the fact that we were wearing our school uniforms. We all ordered a pint of lager or "shandy" (half beer, half lemonade) for the girls and began our experiment with alcohol. We all pretended to like it and revel in the feeling of being an adult. But what happened at that mid-day gathering was to shape my life for a long, long time to come.

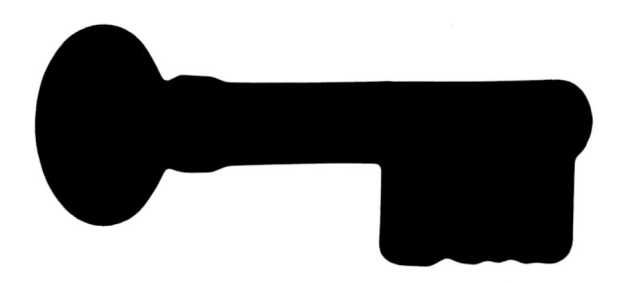

That single pint, (actually more like three for me--since I finished off what others couldn't,) did something magnificent inside of me. It wasn't just that it made me feel a little giddy and happy, which of course was nice. No, it did far more than that. From my very first swig, it seemed as if my problems began to magically evaporate. It was as if, suddenly, it didn't matter that I was in the middle of these very important exams. Suddenly, it no longer hurt that the girl sitting two rows in front of me didn't seem to acknowledge my existence. Suddenly, I didn't have to worry about which college to attend.

In an instant, I stopped caring about the possibility of having to move back to Holland and the inevitability of once again leaving all my friends behind. With a few sips of alcohol, all my troubles began to melt away. It was as if, as soon as the alcohol hit my stomach, something stirred within me, and it began to appear that everything was just fine with the world. I liked how alcohol made me feel. I told myself that I must do this more often. And that moment in the pub was the onset of a lifetime of chasing that elusive feeling to the end of the world and back. At times, I have come close, but it was never as good as that first time in "The Woolpack."

Despite my newfound drunken stupor, I somehow managed to get through my exams just fine. The only real hiccup was that I had to frequent the bathroom several times during the afternoon sessions. But I mostly blame my tiny Asian bladder for that. My test results were less than spectacular, but then I certainly didn't expect them to be anything else considering my utter lack of preparation for them. To me, the test results were good enough to continue my education, and that was enough for me.

Exams were difficult, but I didn't let them get the best of me. However, I couldn't say the same about situations beyond my control. My parents were determined to ruin my life, at least that's what I thought at the time. I quickly learned that my worst fear was about to be realized. My father explained that we'd be moving back to the Netherlands for his work. In a single phone call, my life was once again, uprooted just as I was becoming comfortable with where I was. It felt like whenever I was getting adjusted to life, it wanted to change the rules on me. But I had decided to keep going, and to make the best of my situation—no matter what.

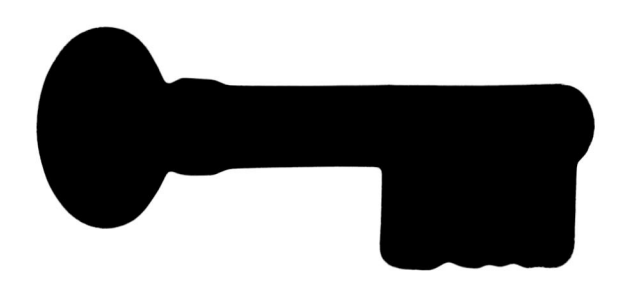

Back in the Netherlands, I joined the local rugby club where I would find my kind of friends. Here there were other men that liked taking their aggression out on the field. Chaps who liked to drink alcohol and party as forcibly as they tackled. Chaps, who like myself, didn't mind being stupid in front of others. To put it simply, these were my kind of people! Whenever I was at the rugby club with these friends, I would completely forget about the awkwardness I felt at school, and at home. This was especially true after training or a scheduled match, when we would gather in the bar at the clubhouse. As a result, I found myself on autopilot for most of the week, but I really came alive on the weekends for sports and drinking with my friends.

Growing Up

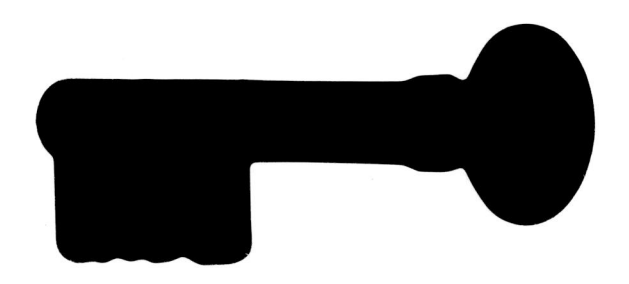

The next several years were like this. I studied; I played rugby on the weekends; I traveled to England to visit my old friends; I found a pretty girl in England; I went into the army; I moved to England; I studied; I married that girl; I worked; I squirted in a daughter; I still played rugby on the weekends; I worked even harder, and I still ended up divorced from my first wife. It would be fair to say that my priorities were not aligned with hers. Work was my life's focus, because it meant money, power and social acceptance.

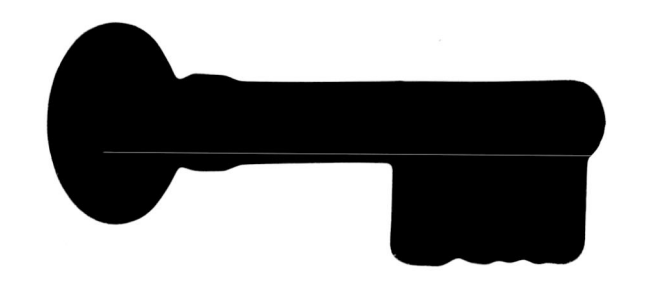

CLIMBING THE LADDER

I'm still not entirely sure how, but at age twenty-four, I managed to get a job at the world's largest bank (at that time.) I landed a position working in the most profitable, high profile department of the bank, where I was involved with some of the most exciting work in the industry. I must admit that I did my part to get there. I was often at work two hours before I needed to be, learned very quickly, and always sought new ways to improve workflow and outperform my peers. It wasn't rare to find me leaving the office two or three hours after my colleagues. I would use that time constructively to familiarize myself better with systems, software, and procedures. I also made a very conscious effort to be the kind of person that my colleagues wanted to be around. I remembered how it had worked so well at my first job that I made sure that I

Climbing The Ladder

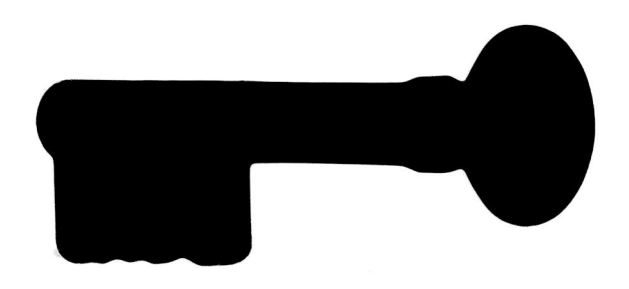

always had my "game face" on. I quickly figured out that when you are given an opportunity and you are busy climbing the ranks, you would make your fair share of mistakes. I probably even used up someone else's fair share, but when your colleagues like your attitude and helpful nature, your mistakes are forgiven fast. By learning quickly, I would reduce future errors, making me more proficient so that I could become indispensable. I always made sure that my bosses were ever impressed by my willingness, hard work, and innovation. That approach has never failed to bring me success in the workplace.

I quadrupled my salary in four years, and my bonuses were now often larger than my base pay. I was going places. I had started off as an assistant to the head of the desk and moved into a junior trading role at one of the most influential trading desks in the world. We traded almost any kind of financial instrument in any kind of currency as long as liquidity would allow us to do so "in size." The size of our trades clearly made up for any inadequacies we had in other areas. For the first time, I was beginning to see that my hard work was paying off. I changed companies and changed responsibilities, seemingly at will. Career wise, I had the freedom to define what I wanted to do and who I wanted to become. In time, I was asked to manage departments and train people, all the while commanding bigger salaries and performance-related incentive packages. If I didn't like what my bosses told me, I would get up and leave and get an even better job within a week. I had so much confidence in my abilities that I never looked back or wondered why everything was so easy for me. I simply believed that I was the creator of everything good in my life.

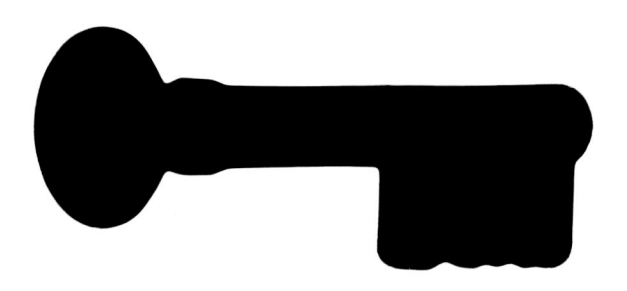

No one else but me made things happen. I didn't have to rely on anyone. In my eyes, I was in complete control. I had a lot of institutional stockbrokers that would constantly try to wine and dine me in order to curry favor and get onto my broker list (a list of stock-brokers with whom I had built a relationship and would conduct business with.) If you were on this list, you had pretty much made it. Trading with me meant that you would earn tens of thousands of dollars on each transaction. In other words, I would be the only client that you would need to become one of the top performers in your office. I knew this, and I exploited it at every given opportunity.

This allowed me the luxury to play the best golf courses, eat at the finest restaurants, and get tickets to the most sought after plays, shows, or sporting events. I had heard stories that some brokers would get their clients expensive hookers and pounds of cocaine if asked to. That was not my scene, but I certainly abused my position as the immature young man that I was. I partied hard with my friends. After all, you have to "work hard and play hard" to be noticed and admired by your peers and colleagues.

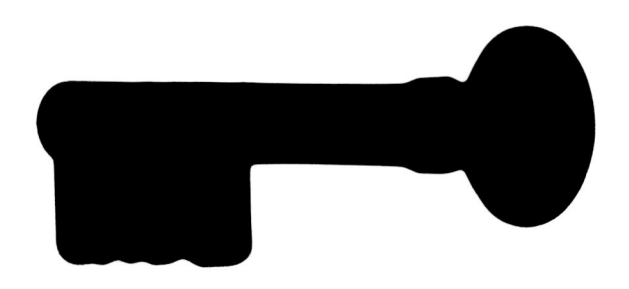

Knowing that a favor-seeking broker couldn't say "no," I would sometimes order a bottle of wine costing thousands of dollars, just to watch their reaction as they felt fear that such extravagance might not be reimbursed by their office. Perhaps, it was boredom on my part and I was just looking to bring some excitement into a life of silly, mindless excess.

In my social life, I dated and lived together with some really wonderful women. I chose well, and they seemed happy to be with me. I didn't sleep around, but none of my relationships lasted much longer than a year. Later, I would describe my behavior as being a serial-monogamist: it was easy for me to fall in love, but I was never able to stay in a long-term relationship. I would move from one relationship to the next, never wanting to commit.

Jai Wurfbain

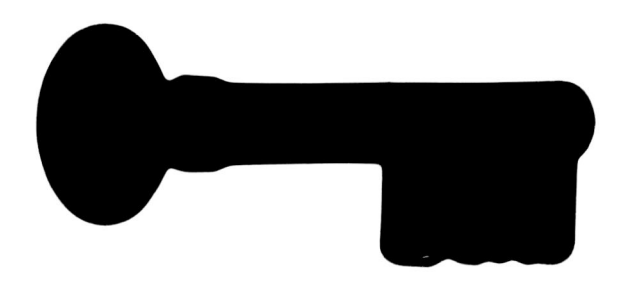

I know now that my selfish needs always trumped the partnership ideals.

I think I was around thirty when, while on a work "sabbatical," I met a very pretty girl in Tokyo. She was a stockbroker working for one of my friends. She had been born in America to Japanese parents and had lived in America for most of her life. She had left New York City prior to her career change and had decided to live in Tokyo for a while. My new romantic target was pretty, intelligent, and she showed interest in me. I invited her to live with me for a while, because I was by myself in Paris at that time. Her boss, the friend who had introduced us, was understandably not overly pleased about the idea of losing her assistant. But, then, what could she do? Who'd turn down an offer to explore Paris? As I continued my round-the-world-journey, I connected constantly with her on the phone. My life sounded like a lot of fun for any young adult and I painted her a picture of a fun and fantastic life. I wore her down with my attention and persuasion. In time, the day came when I picked her up at Charles de Gaulle airport, in Paris, with her three bags of worldly possessions. What could possibly go wrong?

THE FIRST CRASH

When my new girlfriend arrived, I was back working full-time and gone most of the day. What was to be a lover's quest in one of the most beautiful cities in the world, turned out to be dinner for one most nights. Paris didn't have the same pull for her, as it did for me, and we found ourselves as frustrated as a bag of cold croissants. I should have expected this, as she didn't speak French, which made it excruciatingly difficult for her. In order to simplify our lives, we decided to move to London, where I hoped she would be happier. We bought a nice three-bedroom, top floor, two-level penthouse with a rooftop terrace in central London. It was within walking distance from my office. This time, I was certain that a more familiar city might bring us the happiness we desired. But it wasn't so. She continued to struggle to fill her time while I was working, and things began to grow tense between us. So, naturally, what else was there to do but get married and have a baby? Flawless thinking. Pure genius, on my part, I can assure you. As my new wife became more and more discontent, I became less willing to spend time with her at home. Our relationship began slowly deteriorating, and the love that had come on so strongly had suddenly eroded from our weathering storm.

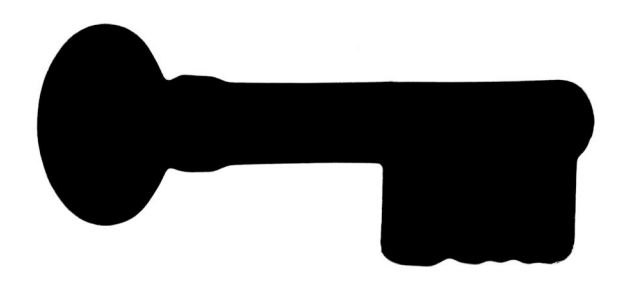

I asked myself, why would I want to go home to complaints when I could go party it up with friends? I would whine to my friends and colleagues about how unreasonable she was, always getting them to take my side. I had suggested to her to get a job, to study for a Master's degree or to volunteer for a charity—anything to get her to stop bitching at me!" Needless to say, that conversation did not go over very well. It was starting to become clear that I couldn't fix the relationship, and as we grew further apart, I started to spend more and more time away from home.

Hope for the two of us, seemed far out of reach. As I began to miss the first days we'd spent together, my drinking worsened as our relationship continued to dissolve. December was always a particularly heavy drinking month for me in my work. Everyone was throwing Christmas parties, and I could always count on a broker to take me out wherever, and whenever, I wanted.

The First Crash

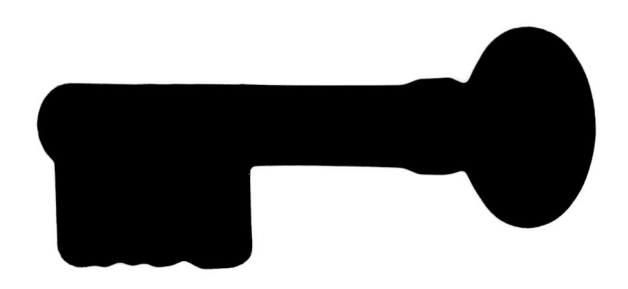

The Christmas season of 2002 was no different. One day, I binged on a particularly heavy liquid lunch and thought it best not to return to the office in the afternoon. I thought I would call my wife to let her know I was coming back to the house so that we could have some much needed "together time," which was something I knew that I had been withholding from her for a while. I started to stumble home as I made that "olive-branch" phone-call. I was just a stone's throw away from the building where we lived, when I walked past a local pub that I frequented in the evenings and on weekends. The open door, the pleasing sound of people chatting, the sound of ice-cubes swishing in glasses and the warmth of a roaring fire seemed to pull me closer.

I hadn't taken but a few steps past the pub, when I heard my name called out. When I looked, I could see several of the regulars whom I knew, beckoning me over. They expressed surprise to see me at that time of the day. It seemed appropriate that I should join them for a "quickie." I vaguely remember calling my wife at one point, later saying that I was sorry, that I was only just around the corner, and that I wouldn't be more than another fifteen minutes. I assured her that I'd be home in time and that she could order dinner out. That turned out to be a lie. Apparently, I didn't come home for some number of hours after. In fact, I don't actually remember coming home at all. To this day, my mind still draws a complete blank about what happened that evening.

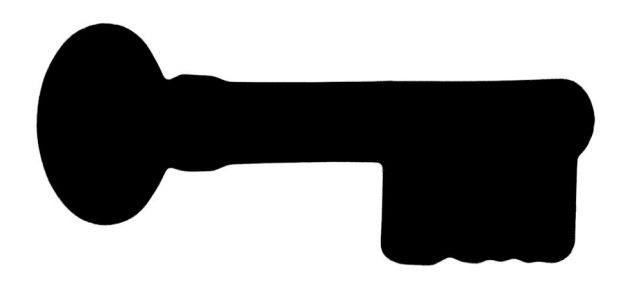

The next morning, I awoke with a terrific hangover. I wanted to call the office to let them know I was going to be "a little late." It was then that I noticed that something wasn't right, and it wasn't just my stonking headache. I went to press the "program" button on my home phone, but instead, I accidentally hit the "redial" button. I saw that the last call from our phone was a "9-1-1" emergency services call made around one o'clock in the morning. I was both surprised and shocked when I saw that. I went upstairs to where my wife was cooking breakfast and asked her, if we'd been burgled or something?

She froze. Her heavy eyes blinked and shuttered for a moment as if they were a dam about to break. Her expression narrowed as she stared unbelievably at me for a moment. My puzzled look must have been too much, as the floodgates opened. I bent down to console my sobbing wife, who was diminished to a pulsating ball on the floor of our beautiful apartment. She tried to speak

The First Crash

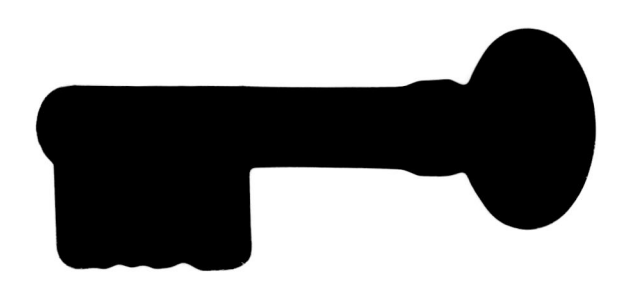

several times before blurting out to me that she had to call the police on me. When I got home from the pub, I had become verbally aggressive and abusive during our argument. She had felt threatened and had phoned the authorities to secure her safety. A typical male, I retreated to the bedroom where I passed out in a drunken heap. The police had come to the apartment to ensure her safety, but they left me alone since I was asleep and had not hurt her.

I could feel chills up and down my spine. I was stunned. I had no recollection of any of this. Even to this day, I cannot remember what happened after I called her from the pub. When I heard this news, I became thoroughly disgusted with myself. I had crossed a line that I never had any intention of crossing.

My adopted parents had taught me to be a gentleman, and I prided myself on treating women with respect. I'd been raised with strong morals that served as guiding principles, which I thought I had always lived by. As a male, I'd been taught that I was to protect women and children. I'd grown up with the ideals of protecting the innocent and never causing them harm. These were unbreakable truths. I never thought I was capable of sinking that low. I was repulsed with myself, and the fact that I was too drunk to remember it.

Jai Wurfbain

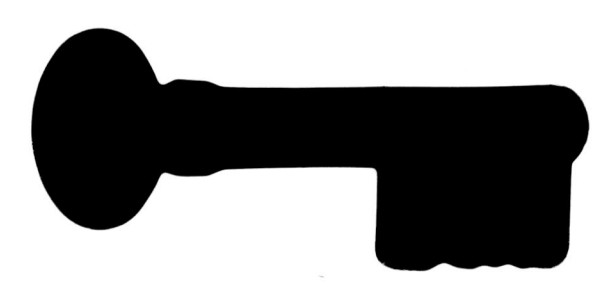

My obvious utter lack of self-control petrified me. The conscious, Jai, would never do such a thing. What on earth had possessed me? I went into the bathroom to get ready for work. What came next was one of the pivotal moments of my life. This was a time when I was confronted with the fear and dread of knowing complete hopelessness. I begrudgingly raised my head to eye my reflection in the mirror. A feeling of tremendous self-loathing boiled up inside me. I thought to myself: *"When did you become such a repugnant little shit?"*

The man staring back at me was such a coward. For the first time in my life, I couldn't stand the sight of myself. I cranked back my clenched first in anger, and smashed the bathroom mirror in disgust. With shards of broken glass crashing around me, it was suddenly clear to me – I could not keep going on like this! My drinking had to stop.

Oh, I had known for years that, "on occasion, I sometimes drank too much." And I recognized to some degree that I had at least some awareness that my drinking was perhaps getting worse. And, yes, there were at least some moments when I recognized that I should probably curb, or at least slow my drinking down.

The First Crash

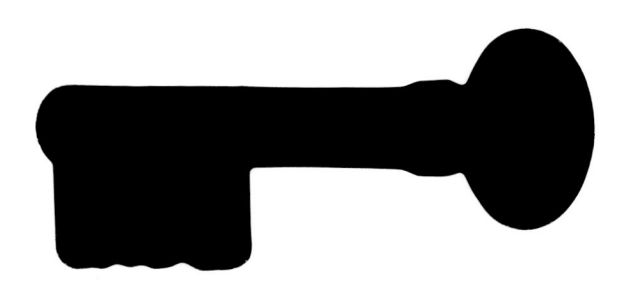

But my efforts to do so never really worked, in the long run. If anything, after these efforts failed, my drinking consumption increased. I had never truly hit rock bottom. I was teetering on the edge, but had never found the hopelessness I felt on that day.

For example, when I was twenty-five years old, I had decided to "cleanse" myself for the entire month of January. It was my New Year's resolution in response to my heavy December partying. I did just fine, and I found it actually quite simple to forego drinking for the month. I felt physically better, rested, and mentally sharper. I liked it. I told myself that I had found the answer.

This was game over, or so I thought at the time. I decided to do that again the following year, but this second time I lasted only one week. The year after, I tried again, but this third time I only lasted one day. I made no further efforts along those lines again. That "take a month off" approach wasn't my only failure at cutting back on my drinking. At one point, I tried following a self-imposed rule in which I would not drink for the first four days of the workweek. (Midweek holidays were an exception of course.) I also tried a "no drinking at lunchtime" rule. Both efforts ultimately failed and were replaced by a "no hard liquor" rule in which I drank only beer and wine, at least during the workweek. Champagne, of course, was "de rigueur" for celebrations and, as a practical matter, appropriate for most other occasions as well. Those were some of my early efforts to get by without alcohol.

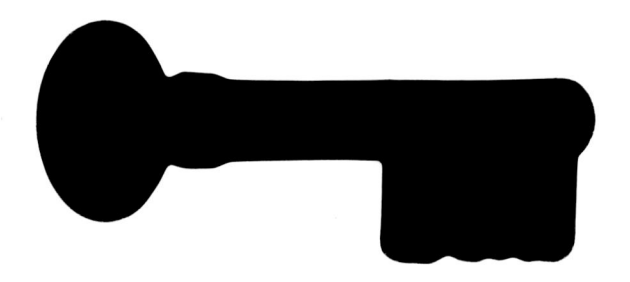

However, alcohol wasn't the only demon that plagued me during those days. Cocaine was also a brief, but pestilent disturbance in my life. The night was New Year's Eve of 2000, on a night when everyone was worried that computers would crash, or Armageddon would ensue, I was tired. Later that evening, I was at a party and ready to go home by nine o'clock. Exhaustion having won the better of me from my month-long December partying—a friend resorted to offering his unsolicited medical advice. Well, come to think of it, he didn't exactly ask. He pulled back my lips and rubbed the powdered cure on my gums and around my mouth. It revived me instantly. My calamity cured, I went on to party like a rock star for the rest of the night.

That episode began a downward spiral into a six-month long borderline addiction to cocaine. It was brief and short-lived--but it shook me up. I never used it frequently enough to become physically addicted, but the psychological dependence was there. I quit

The First Crash

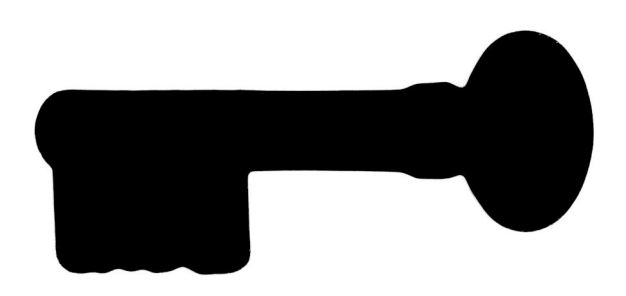

based on my own fear of dire health consequences, and the fact that somehow I felt like I was able to give it up. I knew that even a month more, might mean a much more difficult path out of addiction.

After curbing my appetite for cocaine, I thought I was free from addiction. I mean, after all, I just quit one of the most powerfully addictive substances on the planet. My willpower alone had been solely responsible for me quitting, which fed my ego and resolve to drink even more. I thought that my newfound success meant that I was fully in control, and that I didn't possess the "addictive personality" that I feared I might have. And, so it was that my merry waltz with alcoholism continued unabated for three more years. Those three years gave witness to the darkest progressive deterioration of my spiritual and emotional condition, which culminated on that day when I stood in the mirror. Pure disgust was in my eyes that day, and I knew that it was over. I was finally ready to become free.

A FALSE DAWN

That episode with my second ex-wife was to be my turning point. Seeing myself with shards of glass stuck in my fist, made me realize just how bad things really were. I had finally come to the realization that I couldn't manage my drinking any longer and that I had to face the simple truth that abstinence could be my only solution.

I had totally humiliated myself, and I could very clearly see that alcohol was no longer my friend. I recalled that in the beginning, alcohol was a lot of fun. Then, it progressed to being a lot of fun, but with some unpleasant problems. But in the end, alcohol brought only problems, and they were worsening at a precipitous rate. Looking back, I saw that I had a DUI at the age of twenty-four. But naturally, I had blamed overzealous police work. I had been in numerous fights in bars and nightclubs around the world—but it was always the other guy's fault. I had many terrible

A False Dawn

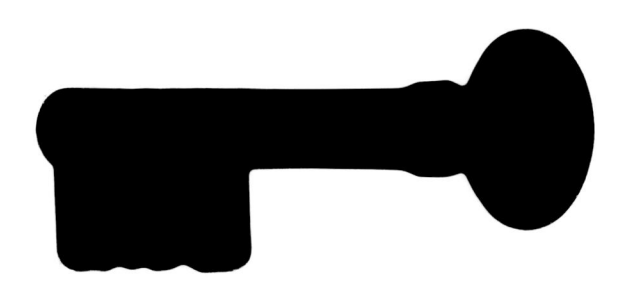

arguments with loved ones that caused temporary and sometimes even permanent separation. Again, these had all seemed beyond my control. There had been numerous hospital visits and wrecked cars. I had never honestly taken inventory for my irresponsible drunk-driving behavior. I was reckless, and continued my drinking despite many obvious warning signs. I always thought that I was the only one being harmed. Others couldn't see it, but I had stopped having fun a long time ago.

Now, it seemed that the joke was on me. Alcohol was masking that feeling, but I now had to confess to myself that the game was up. I later learned that I was then experiencing what is known as a "high-bottom." Essentially, this means that I had hit my rock bottom but did not have to lose everything like many other addicts do. I still had a desirable job, a well-padded bank account, a nice place to live, and a relationship (of sorts.) However, I was told early on by a good friend of mine that I must not compare my rock bottom with those of others. Instead, I must ask myself the one all-important question: "have I suffered enough?" I was told then that, if I had suffered enough, I could begin the process of turning my life around. I was also told that, if I must compare myself to others, it would be helpful if I added the word tiny word "yet" when I found it hard to identify with another person's experience. That small and seemingly insignificant word made it possible for me to relate to all sorts of other people. I hadn't lost my job "yet," or I hadn't gone bankrupt "yet," or I hadn't divorced for a second time "yet." What was important for me to understand, and to honestly come to grips with, was that the answer to that simple question. "Am I done suffering?"

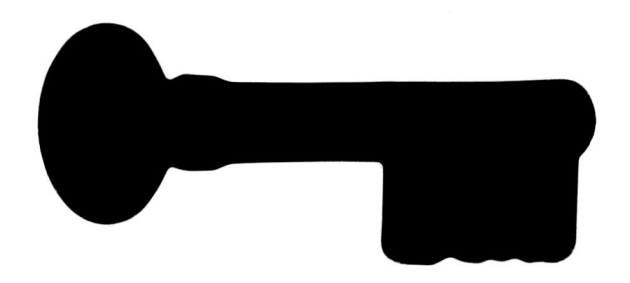

It was vital for me to stay close to my negative memories, not because I needed to beat myself up continuously, but in order for me to keep my desire to stop suffering at the forefront of my mind. I would add that none of my family or friends thought I was an alcoholic, and they were shocked that I proclaimed myself to be one. They all thought that I simply drank too much on occasion. They didn't see the emotional suffering that I was going through. That's because I didn't genuinely let anyone see the authentic me that was suffering. I never wanted to appear weak in their eyes. I never wanted people to worry about me. I didn't want to be a nuisance to others, and I didn't want them to think that I couldn't handle life. In fact, most of my friends and family liked it when

A False Dawn

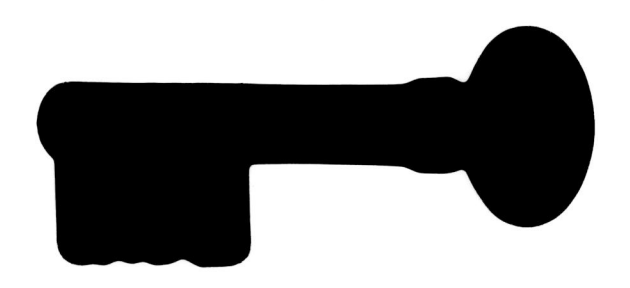

I drank. I became much more talkative, funny, and I wasn't as angry or serious. I liked being liked, even though I regularly told people that I didn't give a shit what people thought of me.

One painful memory was that my parents would always stock up on my drink du jour, having quizzed me weeks ahead of my arrival over what I was drinking at the time. My relationship with them had been awkward since I was a teen and had never mended into something comfortable for any of us. Visiting them was unnaturally difficult for me. But when I was there, after a couple of drinks, I would loosen up and talk to them and even sometimes laugh. My parents were good people. They just wanted to have a deeper relationship with me. Unfortunately, the only way I could really open up to them was through the social lubricant of alcohol. When I stopped drinking, I can clearly remember reading some disappointment and dismay in my father's face. He was crushed, as if he knew that the one connecting medium was no longer an option for us. I was responsible and capable in so many areas of my life, but when it came down to my relationship with my parents, I still felt like that awkward teenager. I needed to learn a new way of communication with my parents. I was looking for approval and love, but I wasn't allowing them to truly know me. This realization helped me to not only learn to love my parents more, but to get to know myself better in my sobriety.

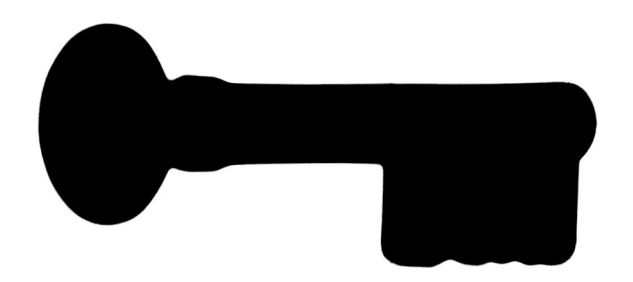

On New Years' Eve of 2002, I had taken my last drink for good. Curiously, at first, not drinking proved to be fairly easy. The craziness of the holiday season caused many people to cut back on their drinking for the first few weeks. It was in my thoughts constantly, that I could no longer take a drink, but my guilt and shame were fresh on my mind. I never wanted to be that person in the mirror again. I was terrified of becoming that threatening, Mr. Hyde character.

In the third week of January, I went skiing in Park City, Utah with some of my ex-colleagues from the bank where I caught my big break. This was something that we had done every year for at least seven years. We also invited Tom, one of our favorite brokers, not just because he was a jolly good egg, but also because we were going to saddle him with all of our very expensive dining expenses. Tom is a very nice man, so nice in fact, that I'd sometimes feel guilty ordering these exceedingly expensive bottles of wine over a two or three Michelin starred dinner. Some cost sev-

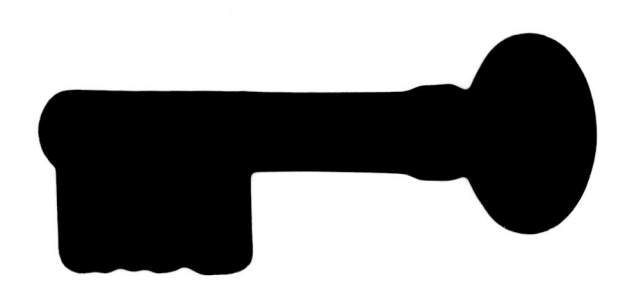

eral thousand dollars a bottle. Understand, that I was not feeling guilty enough not to do it. It was more important to me to show off my power over these people whenever the occasion arose. One other thing that I knew about Tom is that he didn't drink alcohol. He was simply a nice, hard-working, family man who had the misfortune to have his livelihood depend on this little egomaniac with an inferiority complex. We also knew that Tom would leave the house by himself at 6:30am every morning and return at 8:30am with donuts and trays of cappuccinos. We had him well trained. He never seemed to mind being the butt of our jokes and was just genuinely easygoing and delightfully kind at all times. Several days into our vacation, I happened to sit on a chairlift alone with Tom. As we were going up, I said to him, "So Tom, I have stopped drinking as well." He simply asked in response, "Oh, why?" Instead of replying with my usual denial that there was a problem, I told him what had happened in December with my wife. He did not look judgingly at me as I had expected he might. Instead he simply said, "Oh good for you. Are you getting any help?" I remember frowning and looking at him squarely in the eye, saying, "Do I look like I need help?" He replied, "Oh no, that's not what I meant. It simply isn't easy to stop drinking. Have you ever heard of Alcoholics Anonymous?"

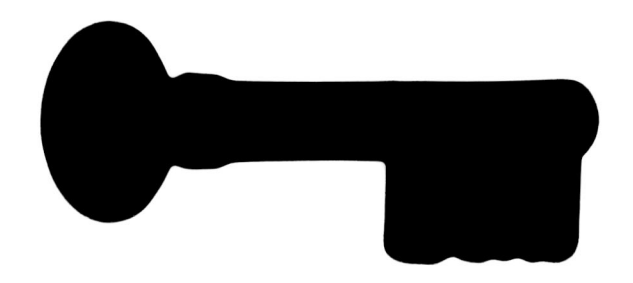

I told him that I had seen some things about it in movies and television programs. I asked him, "Isn't that some cult where they sit around and talk about their problems and then pray about it?" He laughed and replied, "I guess in a funny way it is. Did you know that I have been going to AA meetings every morning for the last fourteen years?" I looked at him incredulously. "Is that where you disappear to every morning?" He confirmed that I was correct. "Would you like to come with me sometime?" I didn't hesitate, replying with a simple "no thanks." He bribed me into going along with him, promising to buy breakfast, which I was going to make him pay for anyway, so I agreed to go with him the following day.

At that first meeting, I looked around the room very uncomfortable and didn't hear much of what was being said. Eyeballs staring at me, *what were they asking me? Why were they looking at me?* I tried to keep my eyes above the circle so that I could avoid their gaze, but on the walls I found something even more troubling: their propaganda. After I read their slogans and their

A False Dawn

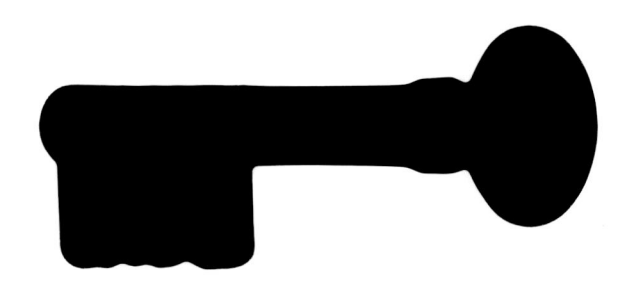

posters with their Twelve Steps and their Twelve Traditions on the wall, I suspected that I had landed in some kind of weird religious cult. There were even capitalized mentions of "God," "Higher Power," and "Power Greater Than Myself," plastered everywhere. I considered myself a full-fledged atheist, and was appalled to see and hear all this rambling about "God." I literally had cold sweats running down my spine as I sat still for the longest hour of my existence.

I grew aggravated as I was beginning to wonder when these assholes were going to ask for my money. Then, right on cue, I saw that a basket was being passed around for what they called AA's seventh tradition (which states that every group should be fully self-supporting declining outside contributions.) I later learned that all of the money went to pay for things like coffee, rent, literature, and the like.

At the end of the meeting, Tom asked me, "What did you think of that? I lied through my teeth. "That was awesome. I can see how that must really work for you!" I gave him my award-winning smile and he replied back to me "yes, it really does, as it has for millions of people." Before I knew it, he was asking me if I wanted to go back tomorrow. I was absolutely dumbfounded, why on Earth would I ever wish to go back there? But before I could object too strongly, I politely refused.

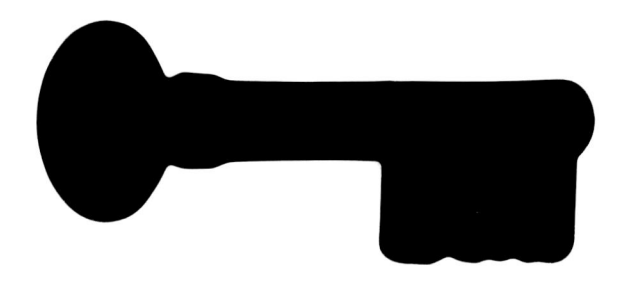

That same evening, I didn't sleep well. Perhaps, jetlag got the better of me, but I was awake at two o'clock in the morning. By the time that Tom got up and was putting on his coat to leave for the morning AA meeting, I was completely bored. And then, out of the blue, my disdain notwithstanding, I started to put on my ski jacket and heard myself say, "Hold on Tom, I'll come with you." I still remember that weird, smug smile on his face.

As we crossed the threshold of the meeting room, I was already cursing myself for my moment of weakness. I sat down and prepared myself for another hour of pulling my own teeth and pinching my leg through my trouser pocket as a way of punishing myself. But as the meeting progressed, I started hearing people talking about being frustrated, angry, and resentful and also something about road rage. These were all subjects that I had difficulty with in my own existence, especially since they were talking about life going on against their wishes and their plans. I was all ears this time. The other people in the room all seemed to

A False Dawn

speak from my perspective. They were sharing stories about how other people seemed to be constantly getting in the way of their own plans. If only everyone did, as I wanted, everyone would be happier. In my mind, I was convinced that I knew better than everyone else what was good for me and for them.

After listening to the others in the room, I felt like we shared the same brain. These people were talking about what was going on in my head every day. Some of them seemed to know what was going through my mind, every moment of every day! Once everyone else had shared, the leader turned around to look at me and asked if I had anything to say. I must have been like a deer in headlights. I just sat there speechless and could feel these very unwelcome emotions well up in me. For the first time since I was about seven years old, I started to cry. I can't remember if I said anything that made sense but I felt strangely relieved at the end of it. When the meeting ended, a lot of people came up to shake my hand and pat me on the back, and they did so without making me feel ashamed, weak, or poorly judged. I remember thinking: did I just announce myself as a newcomer? I realize now that this was a spiritual moment. After that, when an opportunity arose in which

Jai Wurfbain

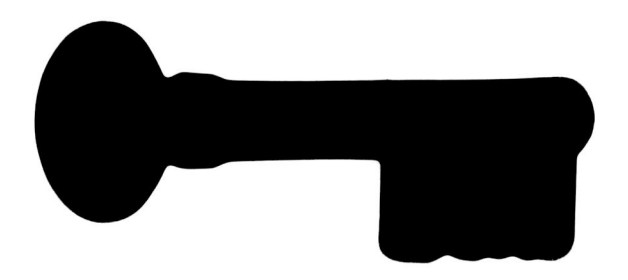

I could catch Tom by himself, I asked him a lot more questions regarding alcoholism, which he answered for me.

Tom also shared a number of experiences that he had gone through to which I could relate. However, we did not go to any more meetings since we had reached the end of our vacation. On my return to work in London, he would occasionally call me to ask if I had gone to any more AA meetings. I told him I had not, but he didn't push me to go. He somehow knew I would not react well to being pushed. About three months into my new post-booze life, I was struggling with something. I can't remember exactly what. It could have been anything at that point in my life. I was wrought with difficult circumstances at that time: my failing marriage, not seeing my young daughter and my newborn son enough, or my ever-growing work pressures. Like I said, it literally could've been anything. Tripping on the pavement would have been enough. I phoned Tom for moral encouragement and he suggested I find a local AA meeting to go to. I ended up going to one outside the immediate area where I lived and worked. After all, I thought then, I didn't want anyone to recognize me. It did not occur to me that anyone who would recognize me in an AA

A False Dawn

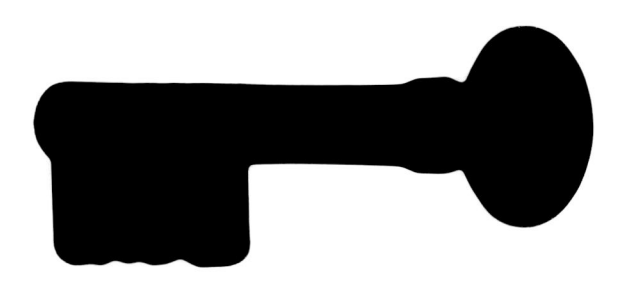

meeting would have long known that I had a drinking problem.

Once again, I began hearing similarities. I had the same sense of relief at the end of the meeting, which gave me the strength to face my problems again. I wasn't a regular, but I wasn't sparse either. I attended when I needed to, but I always made sure that I kept my feelings to myself. I couldn't risk becoming too vulnerable.

My life continued to go on day by day, with and without the meetings. My relationship with my wife didn't improve and I was still unhappy. Despite how bad I felt, I still wasn't drinking. I continued to be angry and frustrated with everyone around me. If anything, it got worse since I had no outlet to vent my frustrations. I later learned that, in this period, I was "dry," not sober.

"Dry" alcoholics are difficult to live with, and that was certainly a fitting description. My wife and I did try to go to marriage counseling, though this was doomed to failure since we were both selfishly expecting the counselor to take our own side and tell the other that they were at fault. I always felt that I had done a sterling job at manipulating the counselor into believing that I was perfect. Seeing my part in all the negative things in my life was still impossible. I thought I was getting a grip on my alcoholism through abstinence, but I was still raging in my "ass-holism." If anything, my unhappiness became more profound affecting all of my relationships.

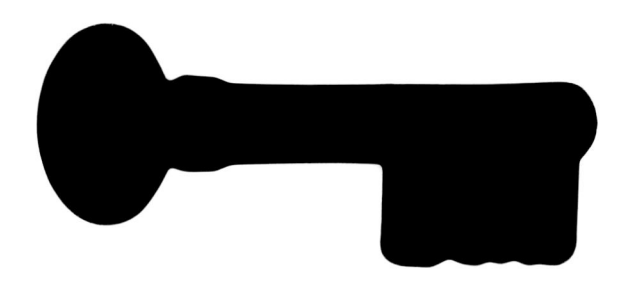

NEW DEPTHS

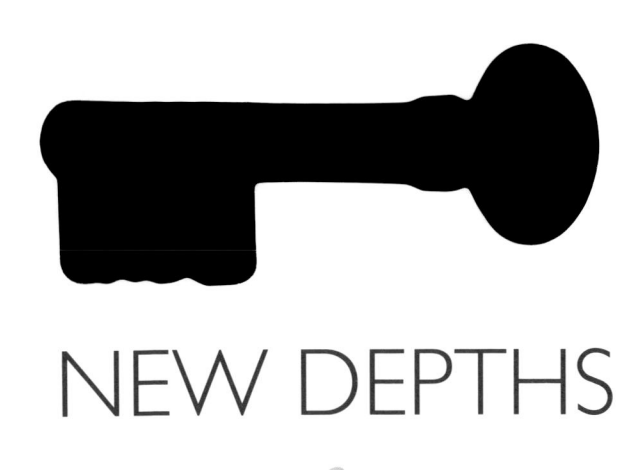

My wife's disillusionment worsened as nothing changed in our relationship. She wanted out badly and wanted to move back to the United States. I knew that there was probably an element of her fearing custody issues over our son, Jamie. She also feared being stuck in the UK because of their existing international agreements to protect children. Staying there meant that she would have locked herself into a country where she had very few connections. I felt guilty, letting her take my son, Jamie, and relocate to the United States. Meanwhile, we continued to work to save our relationship. I knew the risk, but I was in an internal battle of feeling guilty about wanting to make things right for her, and trying to still do whatever I wanted from my own self-centered point of view. She had always been an excellent caring mother and, deep down, I knew that I was too self-absorbed to be the father that I wanted other people to believe I was.

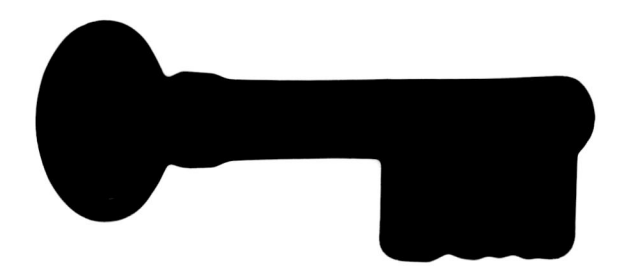

I felt hopeless about the entire situation, when my wife chose to move back to New York City. So, I began working on plans to somehow relocate to the United States, myself. I was powerless to change her mind. Thankfully, the company that I worked for was gracious enough to give me a desk in New York, and to go through the trouble of helping me apply for a work visa. This allowed me to manage my business and the people working for me in London from afar. This was an absolute godsend. The office in London was sympathetic to my plea in trying to save my marriage and they were rather accepting of my antics, despite me beginning to become a "high-maintenance" employee. Looking back, I was making them a modest amount of money, yet was acting like I was rock star. I hope Karma treats them right—they sure put up with enough of my bullshit. Shortly before I was to move out to New York, my wife and son had found a place to live in nearby Greenwich, Connecticut. I moved to Manhattan for convenience to get to work and visited them both on the weekends. Those visits were straining for all of us, and when I threatened to move to Greenwich with them, she promptly decided that she wanted to live in San Diego again. I got the message. I needed to stop chas-

New Depths

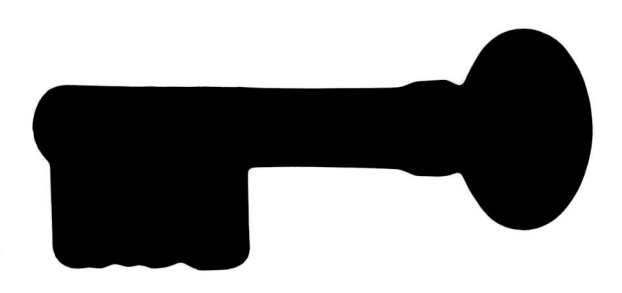

ing her. She didn't want me to be around her, or our son. I had done enough to ruin their lives.

Everything was "fine." I didn't drink, I went to AA meetings more frequently, and enjoyed being in NYC as an expat. But my European banking hours were making life difficult. Waking up early was hell, and my tiredness was bleeding into my performance. I would start my workday at two am, and finish my workday at 11:30am. That year, I didn't make much money for the bank, which subsequently meant that I didn't make much money for myself. My selfish antics were becoming hard to justify. I was going to have to make a change, and fast.

My inability to have a semblance of humility caused me to be aggressive to my bosses in explaining what was going on, and I must have appeared like a loose cannon. At some point, I even told them that my trading positions were bigger than the combined risk positions of the rest of the bank and could easily blow up the bank if they didn't back off and let me manage it how I wanted. At that point they sensibly started to unwind their risk, and I knew that being laid off was just around the corner. I tried to make it look like it was a mutual decision, but no manner of ignorance is great enough to not see what was honestly going on. My ego was blown out of proportion. But I told myself that I had enough money in the bank to do whatever I wanted, and that I was smart enough to make anything I did a success.

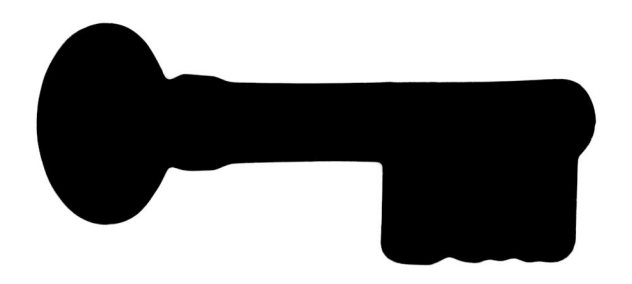

Back when I was still in England, shortly after my ski vacation in Utah, I happened to be bored at work one day and was on eBay trying to find ridiculous things to buy. Not so much out of desire, but more out of entertainment. I happened across listings for properties and land for sale in the United States. This piqued my interest and I looked for areas that I knew, to see what "bargains" I could find. I looked up the area near Park City, Utah where I spotted a listing for an acre of land 25 miles outside of Park City for $10,000. I looked up what an acre was, and when I saw that it was about the size of a rugby pitch, I bought it *sight unseen*. Compared to real estate prices in London or New York, it seemed to me that they were giving it away. About six months later I went to visit it, harboring a lingering fear that I had been conned. When I arrived, I found that my concern was not justified. The property had an amazing view over this green valley with the Wasatch Mountains as a backdrop.

New Depths

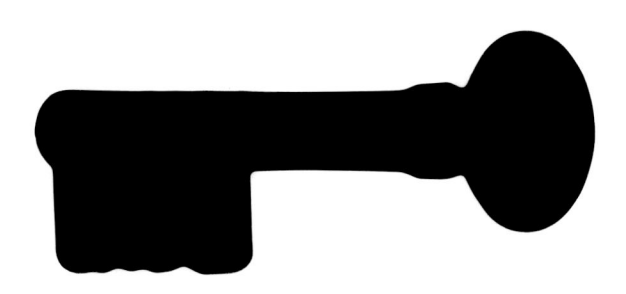

It felt like I had just bought a piece of paradise. I roped a couple of friends into building a "holiday home" together which was, in fact, only going to be used for a couple of weeks out of the year, but would be a great way to stay connected in our small group for a very low cost. The house that I designed was going to be pretty damn amazing. It must have looked truly odd to the builder to meet this strange little Asian chap, with a posh English accent, asking to put up a nice house on this plot of land.

When my work-life started to unravel, I was experiencing a midlife crisis. I was beginning to bring to the forefront of my mind questions that had always been lurking in the shadows of my being. *What was my purpose in life? Why had I failed? Would I ever make it back to where I was?* I desired a restart, a fresh beginning, and to do something completely different. So, needing some fresh air, I decided to move to Utah. My idea was to live comfortably in that holiday home for a while, continue my journey of self-discovery and open a restaurant as a hobby—something I had absolutely no prior experience with. *What could possibly go wrong?*

Now, I loved eating, I loved cooking, and I loved being sociable with people around food. I had all of the hallmarks of a restaurant owner, or so I thought. With the help of some friends, I thought up an interesting new restaurant concept. Thus, I opened my first small restaurant in Utah. It had a unique look and a fun concept that would lend itself nicely to possible expansion. The fact that my menu was out of place proves my own arrogance. But again in thinking that I knew better, despite having friends tell me otherwise, I opened up a restaurant that was completely unfit for its location. It was different enough to see some success in its first year, nonetheless, and people were talking about it in good ways.

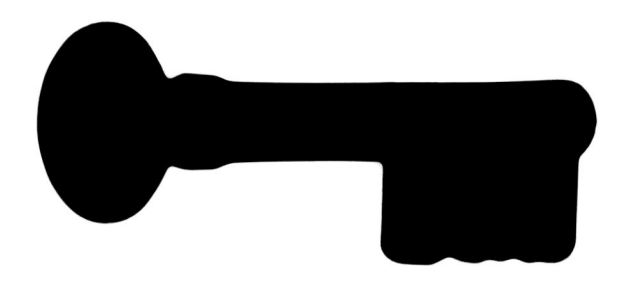

At the beginning of its second year in business, however, the economy took a nosedive due to the recession. Business was slowing down drastically as the whole US economy was in recession. It appeared that outside circumstances were stacking against me, and things were about to go from bad, to even worse. One day, when I was checking my bank account, my world came crashing down around me. My account was empty. Looking back, the event itself should not have been a surprise. It had been in the making for many years. Decisions that were undertaken almost a decade before, out of greed and fear, had evolved into the situation in which I now found myself. My greatest fear had come to

New Depths

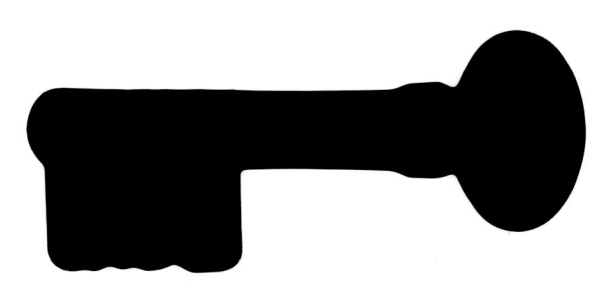

fruition: all my personal funds were lost overnight. For the first time in my life, I felt completely powerless.

This was not just a momentary powerlessness—this was long and enduring. This was a feeling that I was not used to. This was a true shit-storm! I had, of course, endured moments where things had not worked out for me before, but this time was very different. All my life, I had found that things somehow always worked out in the end. Hard work, common sense, and strong moral ethics were the key ingredients to success, or so I had been led to believe.

I was finally able to see that I was powerless over my situation and I began to feel very hopeless about the trajectory of my life. It wasn't that I had always gotten my way, but never until now had I felt such a permanent inability to find solutions to a problem. Either that, or I had rationalized that the problem was so small that it was easy for me to let go of the outcome. This time, my feeling of hopelessness was compounded by the fact that I felt alone in my predicament.

I was very embarrassed that I had allowed myself to get into this big financial mess. Of course, embarrassment was a key factor in not being able to reach out to friends and family. Furthermore, I did not believe that I had anyone in my community who was able to help me financially. I could not think of anyone who had the available funds I needed or the willingness to lend it to me. I didn't feel that there was a point in even trying to bring it up to them. After all, there was still a concern that people might think poorly of me and judge me, which was the last thing I wanted.

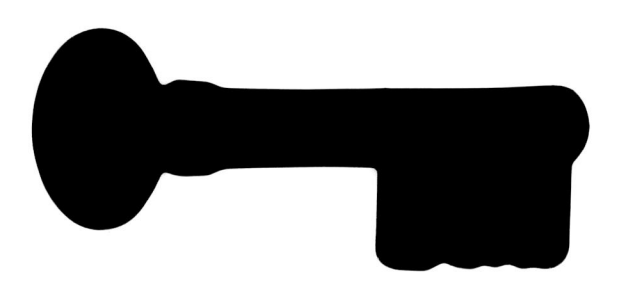

Pride kept me separate from everyone that I knew. It gets me isolated, and hurting. I was lonely, and I felt hopeless. Pride is a funny thing. It lifts us up when we are in charge of life, and it keeps us down when we don't have hope. It can keep us from the people we love, and it can even force us into a holding pattern. I either chose not to connect with the people in my community out of pride or out of my perceived belief that they wouldn't be in the position to help me. All of my friends and family were completely unaware of my predicament. And so for me, pride kept me right where it wanted me--in the same, exact place. Full-blown depression had ensued.

In every direction, my outlook appeared to be dark and gloomy. I felt like I was trapped in a black hole, I so desperately did not

New Depths

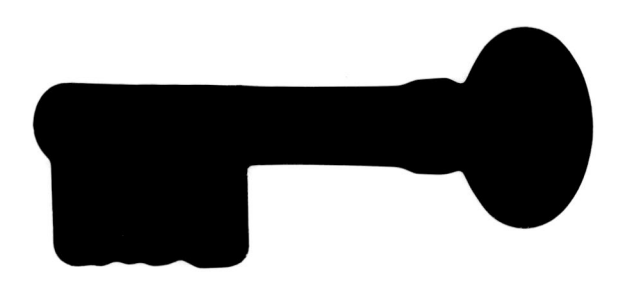

want to exist anymore. I wanted to be dead because that at least would bring relief from my pain and suffering. In fact, to this day I don't know why I didn't go through with the thought of killing myself. I certainly contemplated suicide throughout the day, each day, every day during that time of my life. I was fearful of facing myself, and my situation. Every waking moment appeared to be a terrifying nightmare. My spirit was completely broken, and I had reached the end of my rope. This lasted for several months, during which I ate little and slept poorly.

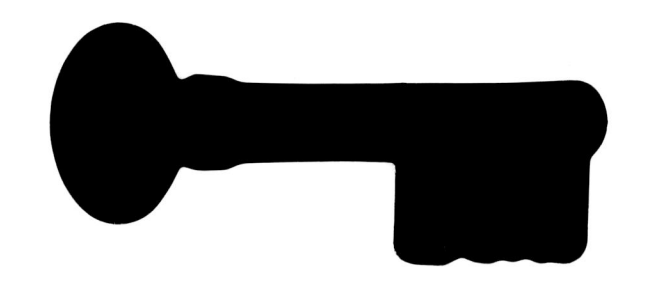

REMOVING THE BLINDERS

I wish I could say that the solution to my deep depression came quickly and suddenly, but that would not be true. Prescription medications weren't an option because I could not afford healthcare. Furthermore, I had never taken any depression medications before because, quite frankly, they scare the crap out of me. I have known too many people whose lives had become unmanageable because of prescription medication. In a perverse way, I am grateful for having to go through my difficulties organically and without medicinal help, because the realizations that I made throughout this period have proven to be some of the most valuable lessons in my life. I don't think that I could have learned these lessons in any other way except through tremendous suffering.

Facing it head on had essentially led me to my spiritual awakening. The suffering that I went through was necessary to thoroughly break me down into a state of submission. Without it, I would never have surrendered my will and I would have continued to rely on my own power. Surrender was never an option in my life. To me, it always sounded too much like giving up. I was encouraged to be dominant, to be a warrior, and to fight as hard as I could. Everyone from my teachers, my parents, and certainly my rugby and judo coaches were supporters of what could be called the warrior mentality. My instructors in the Army were also not going to allow me to roll over when things got rough. Their mottos all revolved around a single idea: you never surrender. You keep trying. You keep going. You persevere. To me, the rules seemed to be abundantly clear: to be successful in business and life, you must persevere.

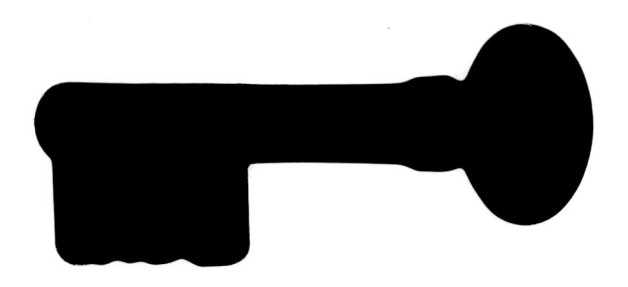

I had been raised to be a control freak. And let's be honest, I had tasted a lot of success with that attitude. It may have all just been an illusion, but being in control, had always worked for me. Yet, in my depressed state, it was clear as daylight. I was absolutely not in control. There was no hope, and I couldn't think of a way out. I needed hope in my life.

Jai Wurfbain

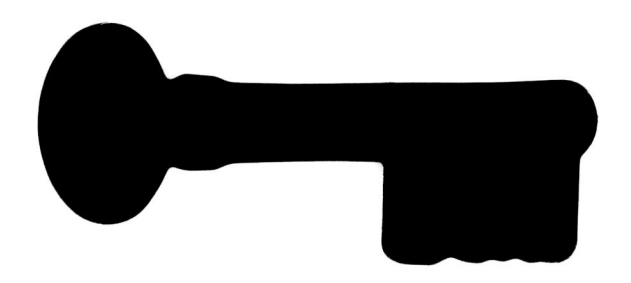

For almost 6 months, I woke up in sweat from my daily nightmares, having had just a few hours of interrupted, restless sleep. I felt despondent, hopeless, and impossibly desperate. I was immersed in darkness. My anxiety made it impossible to eat anything. I had no energy whatsoever. Every night I would go to bed hoping that I wouldn't wake up in the morning. The television became my best friend at night. I couldn't fall asleep without it. The constant background noise drowned out the mental abuse going on inside of my own head. But I was unable to watch anything on television. I was completely self-obsessed, constantly beating myself up with the thought that I had completely screwed up, that I had let others and myself down, and that I was a complete and utter failure. I pondered about going back into trading again, but my self-worth was shot. I believed I had burned my bridges so completely, that I would never find another place where I could work ever again.

Every morning I would wake up sorely disappointed that I had not died in my sleep. My head would continue its cycle, telling me that I was a failure, and that nothing would ever get better. I was completely alone and unloved, and totally powerless over anything in my life. I was hopeless. During that miserable existence, I found it almost impossible to drag myself out of bed, let alone contemplate simple tasks like eating and getting out of the house. I was completely apathetic. I once prided myself on my self-discipline and my ability to keep going against all odds. Basic training in the army had taught me to trudge through bravely, even though every fiber in my body was screaming to stop. I was taught that whatever boundary I reached, I could go beyond that and further. I was taught that when I hit a wall, I would overcome it. Giving up was never an option, but I had reached the point where I didn't even know where to begin.

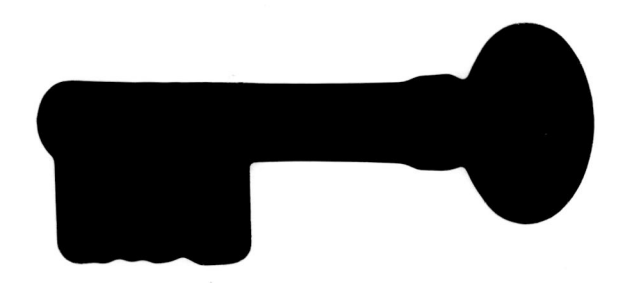

One recurring thought from my loneliness was that none of my friends and family knew how much I was thinking of them. They would never know how badly I missed and loved them. My self-worth was shattered. When you don't love yourself, you cannot believe that anyone else would love you either. I desperately wished that any of my loved ones would call to let me know that they were thinking of me. I needed to feel loved. They wanted to know that I cared for them, and that their opinions were valid. Yes, it did occur to me that I should pick up the phone to call them, but somehow, I couldn't muster the strength. Somehow, that telephone weighed about eight hundred pounds, and I could barely even look at it.

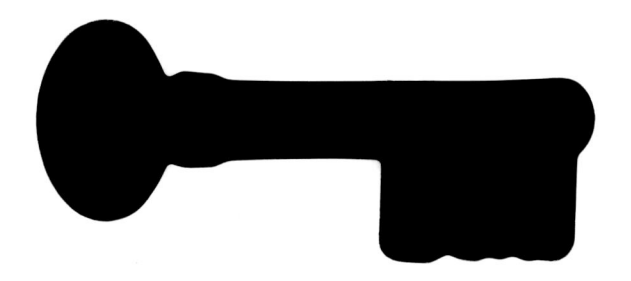

I had been sober now for over six years. In that time, I never genuinely relied on the principles of Alcoholics Anonymous because I always had the solutions myself. Up until that point, I still had never really been powerless, or so I thought.

I started going to AA meetings daily. They became my only safe-haven. One hour of relative bliss where I could listen and hear about the experiences, strength, and hope of others. Those meetings became my sanctuary. I heard how others had escaped from insurmountable predicaments and didn't think that was possible in my case. But, it gave me a glimmer of hope that someday, somehow, things might possibly change for me as well. It dawned on me that the intellectual fencing, which I used to engage about "God," was a complete waste of time. I was too arrogant to recognize my own limitations.

Though raised in the Netherlands, some of my dominant Asian genes led to me becoming slightly geeky and computer literate. Understanding how computers work and relating them to my own brain gave me a breakthrough moment in coming to terms and acceptance of my "God" problem. I was relying on a brain, as amazing as it is, that weighs approximately three pounds and is comprised of approximately 100 billion cells. In reality, this magnificent organ is simply not equipped with enough computational and spiritual power to understand the concept of God or calculate the infinite.

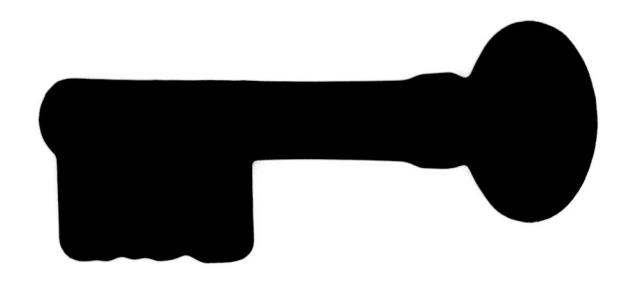

> **"***Pride makes us artificial and humility makes us real.***"**
> ~ Thomas Merton

Furthermore, my brain does not have a very good track record at getting things right instantly, or even at all. Lacking in humility stopped me from any kind of connection with God. I was incapable of seeing the omnipotent or omnipresent because of my own limits. Once I accepted my own limitations, I could no longer deny the existence of God. Now, I am able to marvel at the organization that exists in what I previously perceived to only be chaos. Amazingly, I started to see how each and every cell in my body, from my brain to my toes, are all connected.

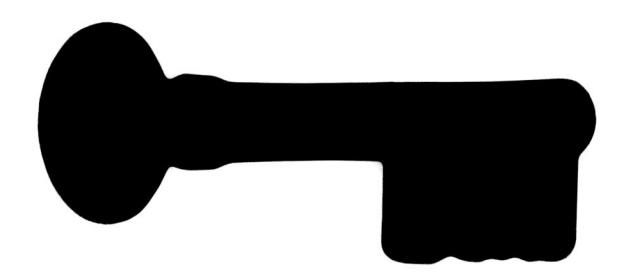

The intricacy with which each cell is a universe by itself is absolutely mind blowing. I know so seemingly little. And that's a great place for me to be. There are three words in the Bible that have always meant something very special to me. I never really felt them before because the remaining seven hundred and seventy-four thousand (and change) confused me. Those vital words are: "God is Love."

That is something I now believe to the very core of my being. Especially, when I remember that love is not always about just getting what you want. Whenever I would waver and doubt the existence of God, those words became my mantra. It was empowering to admit that there was plenty out there that I didn't fully understand. My past efforts in trying to understand God were really me, willing God to do what I wanted. I believed that if I knew how God operated, then I knew how to get what I wanted. It was all a scheme for me to exude my control over everything and everyone in my life. Finally, I gave up trying to understand.

Removing The Blinders

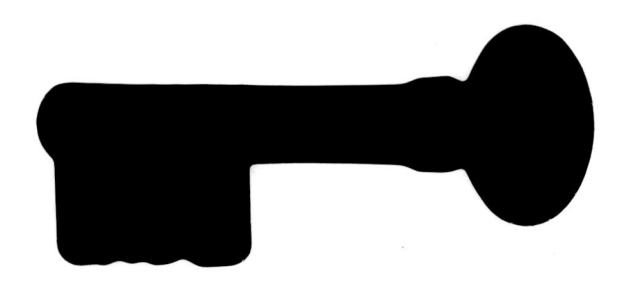

Instead, I began to try to live with gratitude and to feel blessed for everything that is present in my life on a daily basis. When I resumed going to AA meetings, I started to work the Twelve Steps of that program in earnest. The prior reason for why I never fully did that before—the "God" problem—had been removed. I had finally accepted my own limitations, which paradoxically, opened up my mind to new endless possibilities. That was the last piece of the puzzle. I finally recognized that in my mired state of hopelessness, certain thoughts continued to circulate in my head.

"You are out of options; you have no control; you are all alone; everything is beyond your repair; you have no way out; your situation is unfixable; you cannot be trusted; you have been defeated; you are broken; you are disconnected; you are lost; things are not going your way; things will never get better; no one will help you; you are unloved; you are not getting what you want; you are getting what you deserve."

This mantra of defeat went on without end. Looking back on my state of hopelessness, I held misconceptions in three key areas: loneliness, permanence, and powerlessness.

I know today that these were misconceptions and not whole

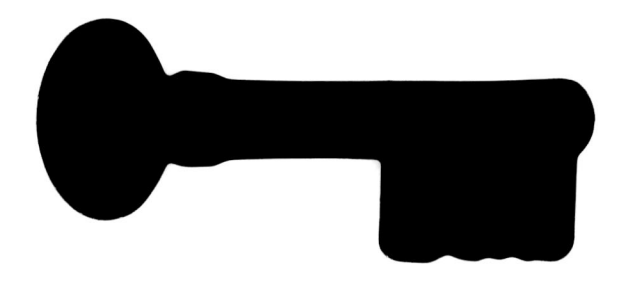

truths about myself. These misconceptions are what trapped me in my hopelessness. My suffering was prolonged because of those ignorant beliefs. I thoroughly understand the purpose for the principle of "hope" now. It is the greatest motivator in our lives. The possibility of a good outcome can drive a person to continue and persevere where otherwise she would stop and give up. In fact, perseverance and persistence are very much dependent on the existence of hope. Even the tiniest sliver of hope is sometimes enough for a person to continue in their quest or goal. History is littered with stories of brilliant inventors, scientists and innovators who were ridiculed by the society of their age. Most scientific breakthroughs and engineering marvels became possible because of the persistence of a single person or group of individuals driven by hope. If no one had pursued the possibility of doing something that was seemingly impossible, our world, as we know it today, would not exist. In the depths of my despair, I felt that I had no hope. I had no motivation to do anything in my life. Basic needs of eating, drinking, and breathing held no importance. If there weren't an instinctual automatic process for these, they wouldn't have happened. I desperately looked everywhere to find hope,

Removing The Blinders

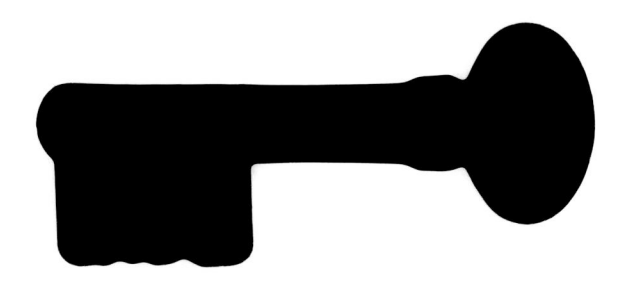

because I knew that I needed something to keep me fighting, to keep on completing meaningless tasks so that I could overcome the seemingly impossible. I needed hope in my life just to get out of bed in the morning. Hope is what made it possible for me to imagine that life could get better, and to continue to fight through the bad times. Without hope, I couldn't possibly even think about getting on a path to success. Going through this helped me to understand the way that the Universe orchestrates itself. I now understand that everything is exactly how it is meant to be. Nothing that goes on in my life is an accident or is without purpose. No matter what chaos or suffering is present in my life, I know today that it is simply up to me to accept it as it is. I don't have to fight any longer. Instead I get to sit back, relax, and bask in the feeling of peace.

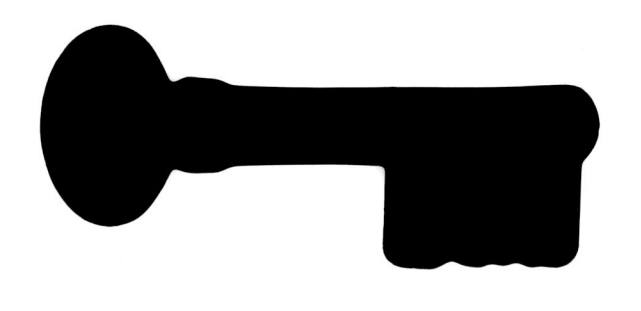

LONELINESS

At the depth of my desperation, I was turning away help from other people because of false pride and an underlying lack of self-worth. This appeared in the forms of shame and guilt, whilst at the same time, a feeling that I was undeserving of the love or even the help of others. I compared myself with others, seeking self-worth through judging another's abilities or attributes as less favorable than my own. I was judgmental. Finding weaknesses in others helped me to feel more confident in getting my way. The old me would search for something that I might exploit so that I could fuel my own ego. I did not like being in a position of weakness. After all, wielding power and being in control is what helped me to built my career.

Another reason my pride kept me isolated from friends and family is because I didn't want to hear their criticism of my imperfections. I got angry very quickly when someone would men-

Loneliness

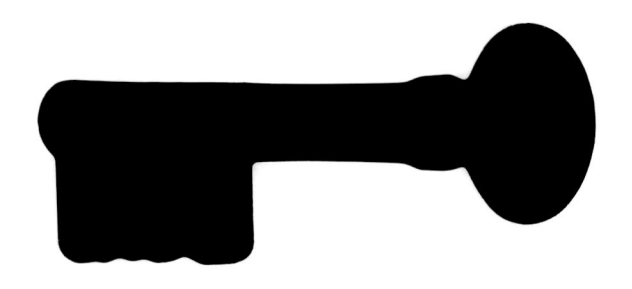

tion something that I had already thought of and would feel they were wasting my time. I would often react sarcastically. And yet at the same time, I feared past errors would be brought up confirming that my lack of self-worth was well deserved. I truly was an "egomaniac with an inferiority complex," as they say of an alcoholic. I isolated myself and in doing so, drew deeper into my spiritual malady. It was impossible for me to reach out to my loving friends and family—not because I didn't think they loved me, but because I felt undeserving of their love. I knew I had gotten myself into this financial mess, and I was embarrassed by my inability to rectify it. I wallowed in my failure to be able to pull myself up by my own bootstraps. I had to overcome this shortcoming before my recovery could begin. Essentially, I had to suffer enough to finally realize that I could not do this by myself any longer. The acceptance of my powerlessness was the catalyst for the most uncomfortable step. Reaching out and asking for help was always hard. Looking back, I now know that I was delaying my own recovery, but this was necessary. Sometimes, you have to go back to truly go forward. This is what I needed to finally let go of my false perceptions of self. Once I found myself in that place

Jai Wurfbain

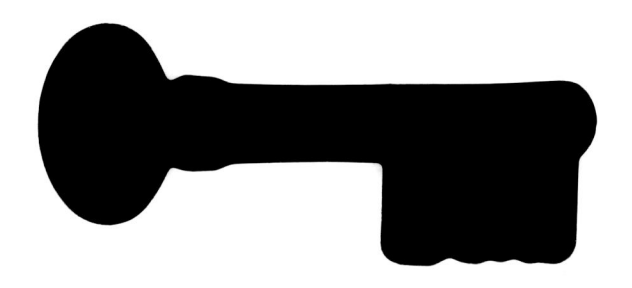

of utter despair, I had nowhere else to go but up. Help would soon come, as I was ready to embrace my mistakes.

That person just so happened to be an old friend from the Netherlands, whom I hadn't spoken to in more than a year. He simply called to reconnect, knowing nothing of my current plight. When he asked how I was doing, I immediately broke down. I began sobbing a flood of tears. I don't know what it was like for him, but it was one of the most relieving moments of my life. All my hopeless feelings and fears were given a voice, and they came bursting through like a ruptured levee yielding to the forces of nature. My friend, Jos, was wholly unprepared for this kind of phone call. His speechless reaction kept me going until I had nothing left inside of me. He allowed me to vomit all the verbiage that described my state of despair without judgment or offering up any solutions. He simply listened in a shocked sense of quiet. He said he was sorry to hear what was going on and how I felt. There was no judgment. He told me he had no idea about any of this, and his words conveyed his powerlessness to change how I felt. This phone conversation had no agenda. It was born from a simple desire, on his part, to connect with a loved one.

Loneliness

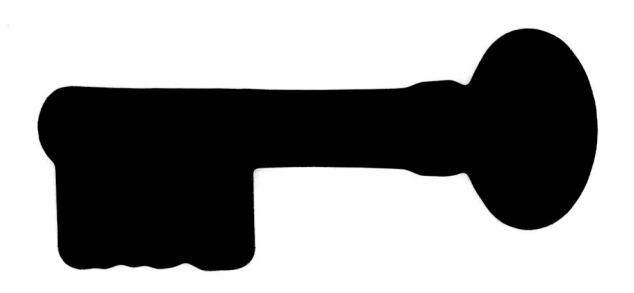

We must have talked for a good hour, and by the time I hung up, I was so emotionally drained that I fell asleep for longer than I had in weeks. That simple, unexpected phone call was a turning point for me. Without doing anything but check in with me, Jos had somehow relieved my suffering. Jos ended up calling me frequently to follow up. When I woke up from my long revitalizing nap, I felt so relieved from that phone call that I made a decision to call my parents to let them know what was happening in my life. I needed their moral support, and I wanted to be honest about my situation and feelings. Later, they told me they had felt that all was not well, but they knew better than to bring it up and discuss their concerns for fear of angering me. They, too, were supportive and actually offered help I did not believe that they were capable of. I had just been proven wrong again in thinking that I knew what other people could do for me. At this moment, I realized that my understanding of the world was severely hampered by my narrow-minded perception of life. My powerlessness was, in fact, exasperated by my own assumptions.

Once I let go of the need to be in control, I recognized that help was there. My pride had been obstructing me, and keeping me separate from my loved ones who were able and willing to help me. I realized that shame and guilt were holding me back from living my life to the fullest. I can't remember having been so ruthlessly honest about myself to another person. It's not that I'm dishonest per se, but I've always been careful how I said things, for the sake of controlling what others might think of me. Honesty is crucial in maintaining a fit spiritual condition. At my rock bottom, I finally was in a place where I was humble enough to ask for help. At this moment, I can't quite call it humility. It was a state of humbleness born out of humiliation. Maintaining a state of humbleness was important for me, because it forced me to care less about what other people thought. The person I have always tried to project—the strong and invincible, Jai, was long gone. All that was left of me was an overwhelmed child who just wanted to feel safe, loved, and valued.

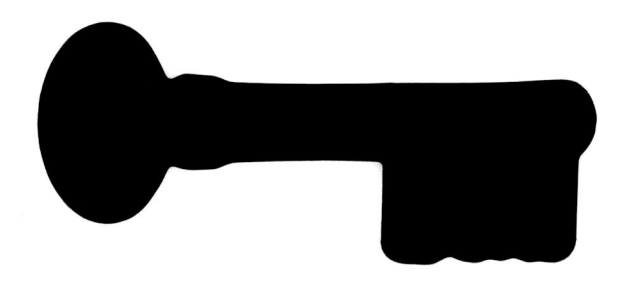

There is, a huge difference between humility and humiliation on the path to becoming humble. Humiliation tends to be very short-lived and it usually leads to the ego wanting to regain control shortly thereafter. The ego will rationalize the situation by suggesting that I was humiliated because of certain circumstanc-

Loneliness

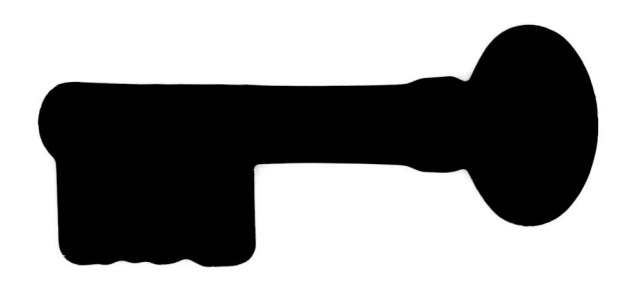

es, and then I believe that I know how to avoid getting into that position again.

On the other hand, true humility comes from the recognition of powerlessness over your life with the faith that you are in good hands. If I was going to make the most of my life I needed to get connected. This is absolutely pivotal in turning your life around. Suicide prevention advocates stress the importance of "connectedness" with others. Studies have shown that social interactions, as well as feeling responsibility to others, are powerful initiators of lasting change. It seems that the answer really is love. Just knowing that you're loved and cared for, is enough to take the edge off of loneliness.

We are after all, social creatures. We are hardwired to connect with others. Our need to belong is powerful and very fundamental. Though my recovery was by no means instant, I had reached a turning point. An exceedingly valuable lesson was learned, and it was a lesson that today I wish to never forget. *Loneliness truly is a lie.*

You are constantly surrounded by the love of others, as well as the infinite love that exists at all times. Understanding that was a breakthrough that helped me begin the journey of smashing loneliness in my life. I love my friends and family. Each and every day, one of my wonderful connections is on my mind. Who am I to say that no one cares about me? When in fact, many people have probably thought about me in the last month, wondering about my wellbeing. How many times have you called someone on the phone and heard this truth reflected back to you? "It's funny that you called–I was just thinking of you." If you can believe the idea that someone, somewhere, has you in his or her thoughts at this very moment, you can understand that you are, in fact, always loved. Loneliness is a false perception.

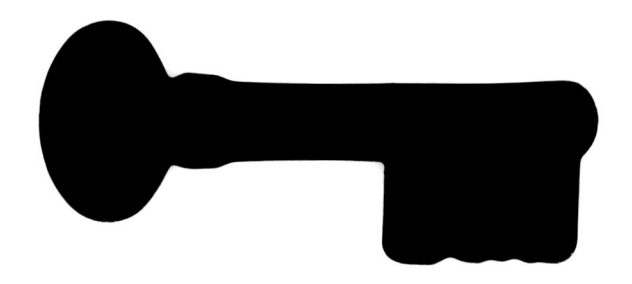

> "*God is love.*"
> ~ (John 4:16)

So, I started to make a conscious effort to combat loneliness long before it became a problem. Today, I make sure that I make daily contact with friends or family. This is in part to keep my-

Loneliness

self responsible to them. That if I'm not in contact with someone sooner or later, they begin to worry about me and ask me where I have been. I make sure that I'm participating in group activities, to feel that I am part of a much larger community. I look to be of service to others, to make sure I get out of the house and out of myself. And it is being out of self that is so vitally important. One time when I was younger, I even felt lonely at my own birthday party, though I was careful not to let other people in on that dark secret. Loneliness can make you so self-absorbed, that you feel completely alone in a room full of friends. That loneliness is created through the disconnection we feel with others. And that is a problem of the mind. The excruciating "awareness" of myself, and how I am situated in the world, had led me to be lonely--despite the presence of loved ones. So again, I must actively pursue getting out of myself.

Today, I don't mind being alone. But I do it on my own terms. I often seek solitude in nature. I love sitting beside the ocean listening to the crashing of the waves. I love being deep in the woods with the wondrous sound of birds and the smell of the forest. I love hearing the symphony of crickets at dusk. I love finding a remote spot away from light pollution to feel minuscule underneath the seemingly infinite array of stars above. That solitude feels amazing. It feels safe and it feels glorious. Loneliness is simply not present. Within me and outside of me, I feel connected through gratitude. It is that connection that is the difference between loneliness and solitude. It makes one miserable and the other beautiful. It is truly only our connection with God that matters.

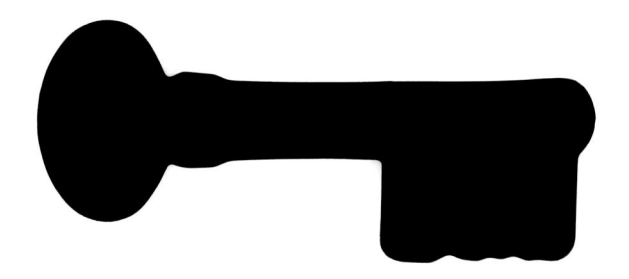

PERMANENCE

During my phone conversation with my friend Jos, I was reminded of the universal truism, "this too shall pass." It was a phrase that my mother always used to tell me when I was sad. But for some reason, in that state of hopelessness that I found myself in, I couldn't see it. It had been a core teaching in my spiritual practice and yet, like the lie of loneliness, I had been paralyzed by the lie of permanence. Impermanence is the principle that everything changes. That everything is temporary and only exists for a finite period. One of the lies I had told myself, as I abandoned myself to hopelessness, was "things will never get better," or "I will never be able to make it out of this."

When I am in this state of being, I am certainly not able to connect to the power of the present moment. In that moment, I am stuck in the past, spinning in the memories of where I went wrong. Regret after regret cycle through my mind, vomiting all over my thoughts. This kind of thinking goes against the universal truth that change is inevitable. Nothing is permanent and everything in this world goes through continuous change. In fact, few things change as much in the world as our feelings and our perceptions. The way I feel adjusts constantly, yet somehow, in the moment I am unaware of this as I get caught up in what is going on in my life in that moment. I am stuck in a vicious cycle of guilt and shame.

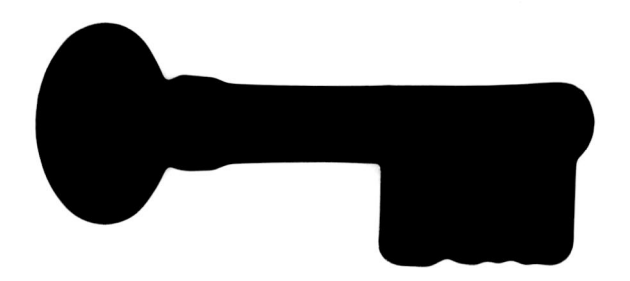

> **"*Everything will be OK in the end. And if it isn't, it isn't the end.*"**
> ~ John Lennon

During that period of desperation, I couldn't see a way out. I felt miserable and desperate for change. But in that moment of trial, I had forgotten that I had always gotten out of my troubles every time before. In fact, my very existence is dependent on everything in my past having worked out. I have had someone tell

Permanence

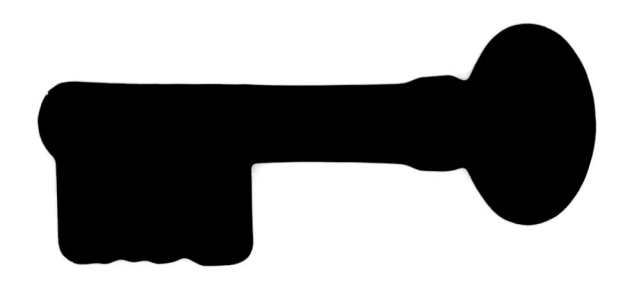

me this before, "God never gives you more than you can handle." This bit of wisdom is the very things that saved me. When I was down and out, I knew that I would never have more than I could handle.

The fact that everything *does in* fact change means that there is always hope for a positive outcome. That simple awareness can give me the tiniest hope to continue, and I only need a little to build on. Remember: "this too shall pass." This simple, wise saying is a tremendous reminder of why I do not have to suffer permanence. It tells me that no matter what is happening in this moment, things will change. This proverb indicates that all material conditions, positive or negative, are temporary. If I can keep this in mind, when some things are not going as well as I would like or even if they are disastrous, I can always remember that nothing stays the same.

The original writings of this saying are from the medieval Persian Sufi poets and, down through the ages, many other great thinkers have applied them. President Lincoln, used this saying as a mantra to support himself during troubled times with his family and during his civil war administration. If it was good enough for

Jai Wurfbain

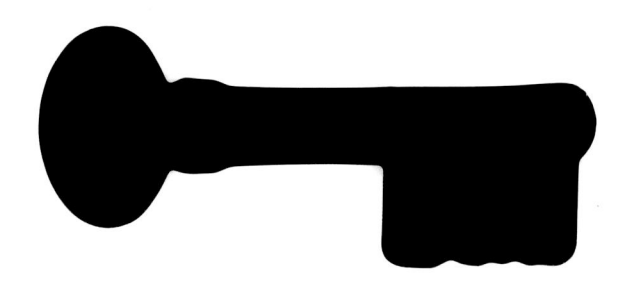

Abe, it has got to be good enough for me. Do you remember your first crush? Though it does happen on rare occasions, chances are that you are not with that person any more.

I was only about seven years old when I fell in love with the most delicious, beautiful girl in the world. Her name was Astrid, and she was as cute as a button. I played with her in and out of school, and if I weren't playing with her, I'd be teasing her. At night in bed, I'd be thinking of her, and I remember my mom giggling outside of my bedroom door when I was singing ballads about her. I was intent on marrying her. When my family moved to England, she was the single largest reason of my unhappiness at that time. How could they uproot my life away from my beloved, Astrid! I wanted to die then, and I didn't think I'd ever heal from that loss. Only I did. I did every time. I fell in love and out of it again. Every time, I was told that "this too shall pass." I never believed it would, but it always did. Every time.

Being reminded that every thought and situation in life is temporary helps me to get a perspective that will support me to work through any challenge. It gives me *hope*. Life is all about change, be it in our personal or professional life, the seasons, or in the

Permanence

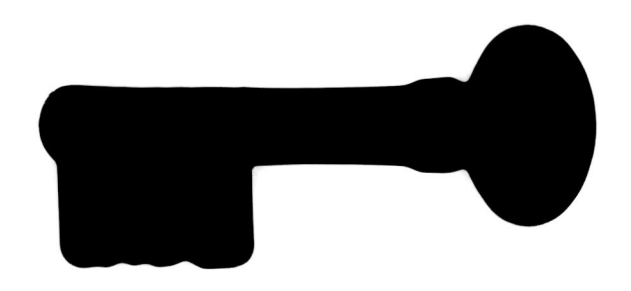

global economy. Hope. It's such a tiny word, but its implications in our lives can change everything. It is the art of knowing that in order to be at our best, we must allow things to happen in their correct timing. In order to be allowing, we must also be trusting. The feelings we have associated with our lives are all temporary to some extent. We can let situations work for us, or fight them when they seem to be against us. It is our choice what we do with each circumstance.

Every situation that we find ourselves in is a single piece of the larger puzzle that we call our lives. We can watch as they happen, or allow them to fit together, and know that we are being served. The powerful influence of our feelings is what can either make us or break us. In order to support us in our emotional journeys, we've also been programmed with highly elaborate mindsets. Our frame of mind is what hope is built upon. When we are struggling with something, our mindset can aid us through that difficult time. Likewise, when we are thriving, the good passes in the same way as the bad. When we recognize that change is inevitable, we can relax and flow with it. This will also be immensely helpful in allowing us to go with the flow as we learn that permanence isn't real. Knowing that life will continue, long past our struggles is encouragement to help keep us going.

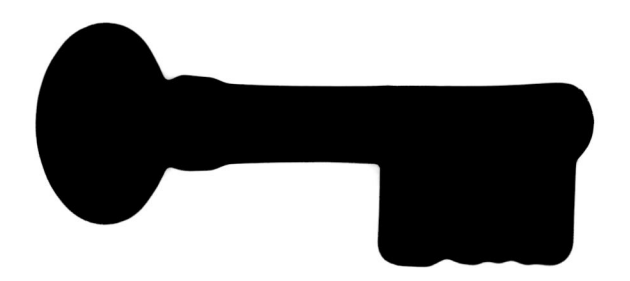

What's the best way to get over the fact that we won't be in the same situation forever? We begin by embracing the idea, and then we learn to accept it. If we don't, we get knocked down as a result of our non-acceptance of change. We can apply this in a relationship, a job, a business, or a loss of a loved one. You will, at times, become sad, frustrated or disappointed as a result. The process can become frightening as you do your best to find your own path and get back on track. The aim is to gain clarity as best you can so that you can move forward towards a positive present moment. I now feel that I am blessed with my life, as it is up to me how I make it happen. I need to have adversity and experiences that will challenge me so that I can be shaped into the best human being I can be. During times of challenge, I am not able to see the big picture of what is to come in the future, so I do not always let the experience happen in its own time. Instead, I do my best to block it in whatever way I can.

Resilience is one of the great character traits that can help us to face adversity. In my journey I had to be resilient, there was no

Permanence

other way to get through the pain. Pain is not weakness. That's a common misconception of our society. We all know that life has its ups and downs and is in constant flux. Moving with it, and allowing life to happen, is a sign of strength. Being able to recognize our pain, and to experience it, is vital to becoming aware of ourselves. Remaining vigilant during these times is one of the most important aspects of faith.

In times of trouble, I must remember that whatever happens will soon change and become a distant memory. Remember: "this too shall pass." In the midst of turmoil in our lives, we must remember this advice to help calm a troubled mind. In that moment, as I hear this message, it doesn't seem possible. It hurts too much, or perhaps the anger still seems too raw. Taking a pause in the disorder of my life to reflect on this wise saying can make a tremendous difference in how I continue to feel, and how I continue to respond to whatever is causing me pain or anger. Let's consider this saying deeply and see how we can apply it in our life to have immediate effect.

I can experience moments of calm even in pain. This fact alone is enough to prove that even physical suffering is impermanent.

Jai Wurfbain

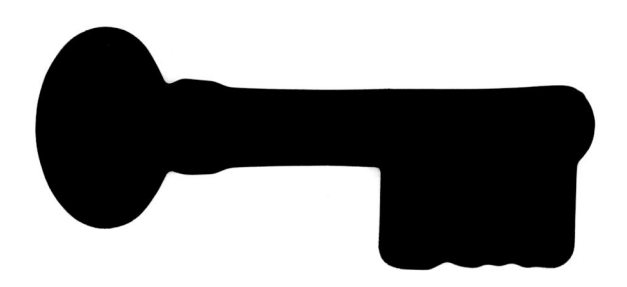

When we are experiencing acute mental suffering, it is not because of something that happened to us but because of our perceived thoughts about what we think happened to us. Our mind conjures up fears and anxieties from our past or from the unforeseen future. The pain we feel is based on the assumption that what is about to happen will be negative. The difference between hope and assumption is that hope plans for the possibility of a positive outcome, and assumption writes it off as already having happened. The bad feeling, and my continued focus on it, is what keeps the suffering alive. Just having the knowledge that we are getting upset because of thoughts, instead of something or someone actually being threatening to us, can be very powerful. Even if at that moment, we cannot see a way to let it go.

In any circumstance, remember that *this too shall pass*. Even when I choose to hang on to the negative thoughts and feelings about an upsetting incident, they eventually smolder and evaporate. This too shall pass. I can bury that anger, grief, hurt and so on for many years, but I can't keep the emotion going forever. It will eventually leave. This is the cycle of life, and this wise old saying cannot be anything but truth, for every moment, good or bad, will eventually pass. It's what I do next that actually causes acceptance or suffering, and even that will pass in time. Sometimes, I can speed this up by taking an action to help it out the door.

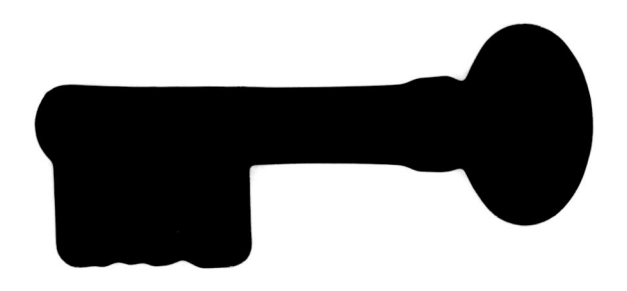

> **"Whatever is, will be was."**

It's important to keep in mind that a moment is just a moment. In reality, no matter what I think about or feel, I am still as I was the moment before. The only thing different is how I feel about the past moment. Each moment passes on in a linear world, so knowing that a moment will pass seems a ridiculously obvious point. But from a human standpoint, a moment of grief, rage or intense hurt can linger on for a very long time if I keep holding on to it. I always have the choice to help the moment pass on. This will allow me to embrace a new moment by accepting the moment as it is, not struggling with it, and simply letting it move on. This moment will pass. The choice we must face is: do I hang onto it, or do I agree to accept that it was what it was, let it go, and pass on by? The next time that you feel that things are not the way you want them to be or that you are upset, disappointed, stressed or worried, remind yourself: "This too shall pass."

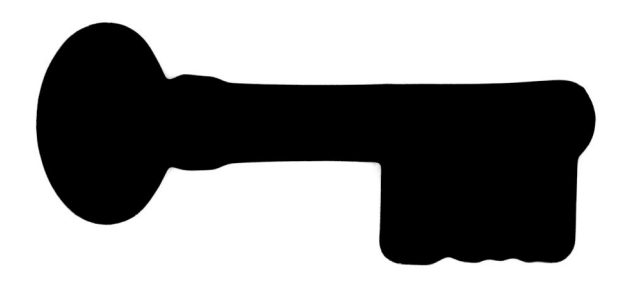

> **❝ HOPE** – *it's not pretending that troubles don't exist it is to trust that they won't exist forever. That hurts will be healed and difficulties overcome. It is faith that a source of strength and renewal lies within to lead us through the dark to the sunshine.* **❞**
>
> ~ Anonymous

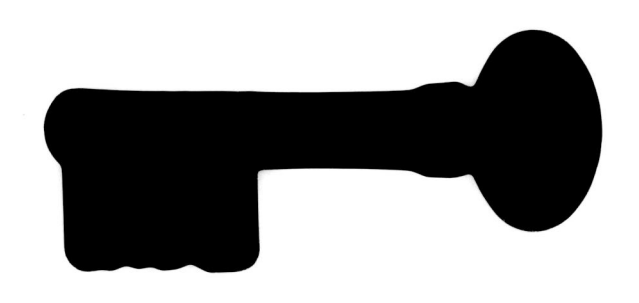

POWERLESSNESS

The third misconception I had was that I was powerless to change my broken life. I was suffering from a gross misunderstanding of what personal power actually meant. To me, power, always meant power over another person or situation. I needed to learn how to take ownership of my action. I learned something profound during this period. Power, in its purest sense comes from "letting go," and "accepting."

For a very long time, I was under the impression that I had lots of power. Then, when that day came that I found my bank account empty, I felt very powerless. I was completely lost. Powerlessness was one of the hardest concepts for me to understand since I had always been under the impression that I made things happen. If I wanted something, I would save the money for it and eventually buy it. If I was interested in a certain person, I would go up to them and talk to them. All of these things gave me the false impression that I had power, that I had control, and that I could manipulate a situation into a more favorable outcome. I began to see that powerlessness is an underlying thread that exists in my daily life and that it is a critical component of fear. Fear could not exist without it. Fear is the unknown, the uncontrolled, and the chaos of life. Hope is what gives us the possibility that, although we have no power or control over something at present, we will have it again at some point in the future. Hope is the only thing that makes powerlessness bearable.

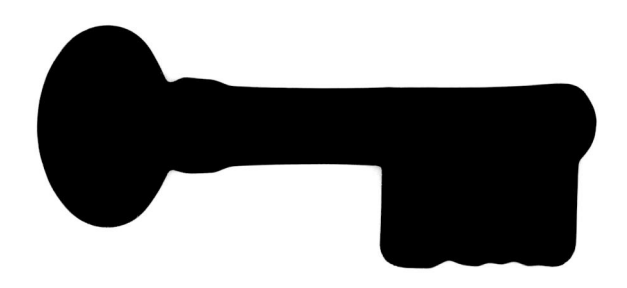

From the moment that I was born, I participated in the ride that we call "the game of life." As a small child, I learned to manipulate the environment around me. Since I was incapable of feeding myself or keeping myself warm and dry, I had to rely on others to ensure my survival. When I was in discomfort, crying would see to it that loving hands would relieve me. Oh, they might try to give me something other than what I wanted, but I would make sure they would eventually give me what I wanted. As I grew, I learned to grasp things with my hands. Some of the things I took in my hands were taken away, but either I would get those things back or be given something even better—but only if I cried loud

Powerlessness

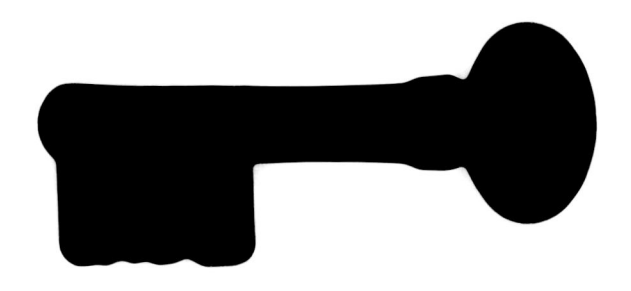

enough. As time went on, it got harder to get my way, which is why I learned about patience. Patience as I found out later in life was simply waiting to get what I wanted.

I have always had the uncommon knack of manipulating anyone or anything within my reach. Paramount to my success were my communication skills. I learned that, as long as I was able to change the perceptions and behaviors of others, I was in control of my universe. There was no room for another power to compete. The saying "if you want to get something done, you'll have to do it yourself," had always made sense to me. I now recognize that my sense of expectation has been a great source of suffering for me. For some reason, I have always believed that I was entitled to a positive outcome because of my hard work. I am good at complicated planning, where I'm trying to achieve a certain outcome in the future. However, it is important to always remember that I am no longer in the business of results. While I may have many options that I can pursue in any given situation, it is ultimate arrogance for me to assume, or to believe that I can achieve a guaranteed outcome. I have heard it said before that expectations are resentments waiting to happen.

Jai Wurfbain

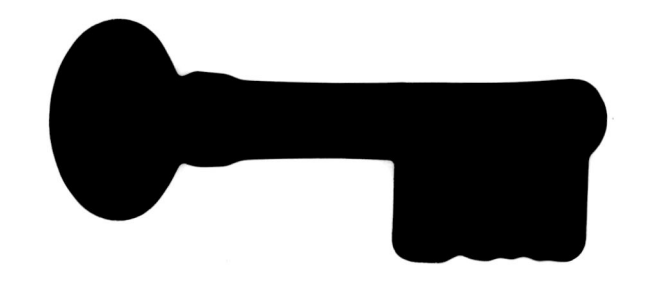

> **"God, grant me the serenity to accept the things I cannot change, the courage to change the things I can, and the wisdom to know the difference."**
>
> ~ The serenity prayer

The serenity prayer is often used in AA meetings. Its three stanzas offer a great source of comfort to those who can actually allow its words to speak for them. The first stanza reminds me to not suffer, or to at least let go of suffering. When things just don't go my way, the first stanza instructs me that I must allow God to take charge. The second stanza talks about doing the things that I myself can control, such as to persevere. I need to keep trying, to not quit before the miracle happens, and to be courageous and hopeful. The last stanza reminds me to be thoughtful and aware,

Powerlessness

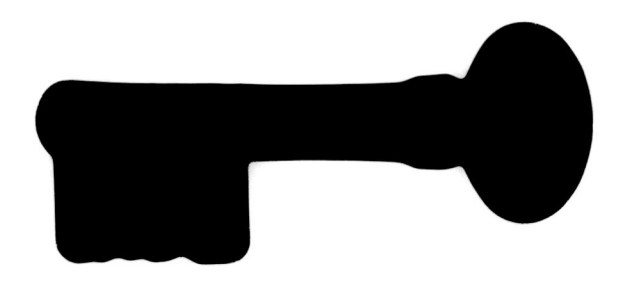

to be open to other perceptions, and to choose wisely between trying to control and letting go. And here, again is the paradox. Once you relinquish power, you actually tap into a far greater power, a "Higher Power."

When I accepted and allowed this Higher Power to work in my life, I made a great discovery. I discovered that happiness and joy foster energy and emotion all on their own. And this energy can come to us naturally, which fosters our inner growth. Joy is a state of non-resistance and freedom. It is nature's gift to help us grow. When we no longer suffer negative emotions and the need to grasp them, in order to survive, then we can release them. Knowing this simple truth, allows me to understand that I always have been, and always will be, in good hands. My own power is nothing compared to that of God's. In that, I have faith and acceptance. Initially, I didn't like the word "acceptance" because my previous understanding of that word was "surrendering" or "giving up." Today, acceptance is what has become my "key to faith." I had to accept my powerlessness before I could accept the help of others. I had to accept the principle of being open-minded in order to accept that everything was going to be just fine without me controlling everything. When I say that I initially didn't like the word "acceptance," I mean that I absolutely loathed anyone telling me to "just let it go and accept it." I was extremely sensitive to injustice, and I would regularly invoke the phrase "it's the principle that matters," to justify my anger towards the events in my life.

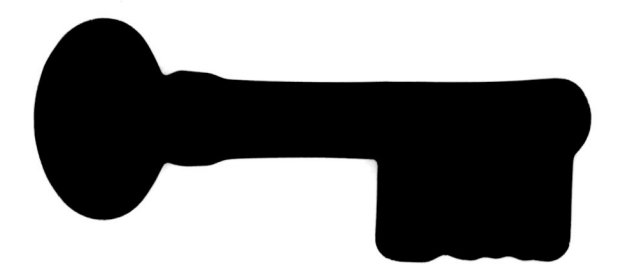

> *"When you learn to accept instead of expect, you'll find more happiness."*
>
> ~ Anonymous

It took a wise mentor to teach me that acceptance doesn't mean that I approve of the actions and words of others. Acceptance is about respecting and allowing others to be themselves when they differ with my own lofty opinions. Acceptance is absolutely necessary to help us find peace. My peace was constantly shattered

Powerlessness

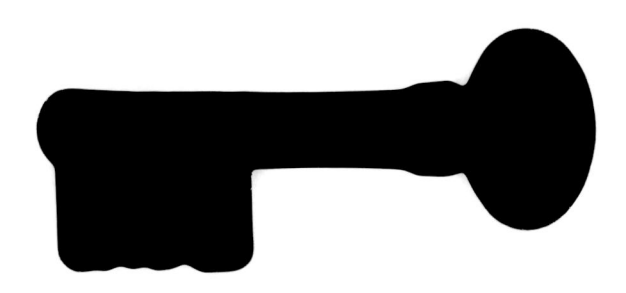

by the competing interests of others, or by inexplicable events that served as barriers to me achieving my expected goals. Those silly expectations are always getting in the way. Acceptance was possible even for me. With a little humility, and through being open-minded, I have come to realize that I'm not the one who knows what's best for the world. That's where God's power lies. It can be found by anyone, anytime when your heart and mind are at peace.

It's important to realize that I knew of the existence of a Higher Power, much earlier in my life. Yet, the wounds of alcohol shut down my access to the source of Creation. This incident occurred when I was vacationing with my wife in Boracay, a small island in the Philippines. The only reason I wanted to go was because I had read in some fancy travel magazine that it had been named as one of the top three beaches in the world. At that time, everything I did was designed to impress other people.

When I got there, I found that it was everything the travel magazine had said it would be. The hotel was magical. The hospitality was impeccable. The sand on the beach was golden and so clean it seemed that an army of people were combing the sand each night to remove any imperfections. The ocean seemed ridiculously blue everywhere, and there was just the right amount of breeze at all times of the day. One evening, just before dinner on the beach, I was looking towards the west to witness the sunset. I remember the image of the glowing orange ball reflecting off the water. It created a picture-perfect golden road that stretched all the way from the edge of the beach to the edge of the horizon and out past the setting sun. I could hear the palm trees sway softly in the breeze, and I could feel the sand caressing my feet, while the water lapped my ankles. At that very moment, I remember thinking: "It kind of sucks that there isn't a God. There isn't anyone or anything that I can thank for this moment."

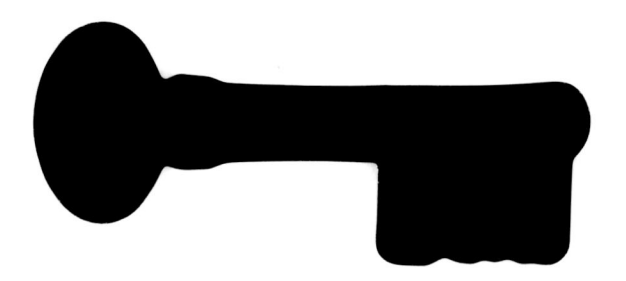

I sat there for a while afterwards, letting sand run through my fingers trying to find God. I looked up at the sun and thought about the trajectory of my life. There was not a trace of anything related to a Higher Power that I could detect, and so I let the sand crash back onto the beach and dusted myself off. My wife called for me to shower and head to dinner. God would have to wait for me for another five years; I had dinner plans.

Today, I have faith. I know that the illusion of fear made me think it was much worse than in actuality. Almost nothing that I feared ever came to fruition. Fear had gripped me and lied to me. The suffering led me to understand that I am not alone and that I am walking hand-in-hand with God. There is no doubt of the existence of a Power Greater Than Myself in my life. I don't have to understand what that power is. I simply recognize its existence and live in gratitude for it. The lessons that I've learned became the foundation for the rest of my life. They were in fact teaching me to be present, grateful and happy at any time that I desired it. I became free to embrace peace, love and joy at my choosing and to not be a victim to fear, suffering, chance or destiny. I learned that I have a choice between, "When everything works out, I will have peace" or, "When I have peace, everything works out." When I first heard others say that they were "grateful," I certainly didn't believe them. I thought they were lying or delusional. Probably both. But here I am today, grateful for my "gift of desperation."

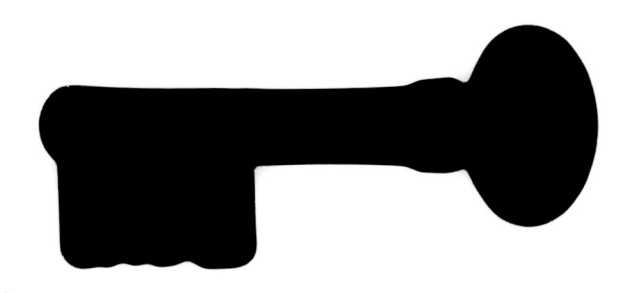

It was desperation that led to the suffering. Suffering gave me the willingness to change, and I now know what the phrase, "If I had gotten what I wanted, I would have short-changed myself" means, from the bottom of my heart. A good friend of mine often shares, "I have so many blessings in my life that I never saw coming." I feel the same way, and our heart warms when we recognize the miracles in each other. She recently got engaged with a man with whom she connects so deeply, that it sends shivers down her spine. This is a very different state of being compared to some time before that, when yet another relationship came to an end for her. She had fought to keep that relationship going and tried anything in her power to do so. But it simply wasn't meant to be.

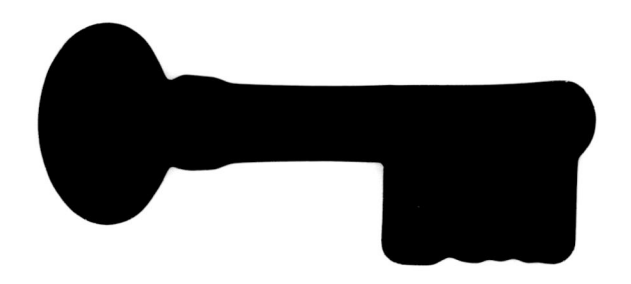

To feel blessed is to see the miracle of not being in control. To let go of power is to move from suffering into love. She could never see it coming, because she did not orchestrate for this to happen. She moved from hope to faith with the awareness of that miracle.

A SECOND WIND

Once I had that tiny glimmer of hope back in my life, it was important to keep it alive. I was well aware I would continue to have emotional ups and downs, but I did not want to fall back into the same downward spiral as before. Despite being a little jaded, I decided to take action. It wasn't a regimented "program of action," but small steps that I could use to measure my progress in the right direction. The things I was unable to do because of my debilitating depression were again made possible through the energy of hope. Before, it was almost impossible to get out of bed. Hope made it easier. Simple tasks that were painful to even contemplate before, I no longer avoided. The importance of doing the little things is immense. Having a really long shower became a therapeutic experience. I would be contemplating emotional and spiritual cleansing as I was giving myself a thorough scrubbing. With my newfound hope, I would think of other people I could call and let them know what was going on. I reached out with more comfort and ease and would not let pride get in the way of people helping me.

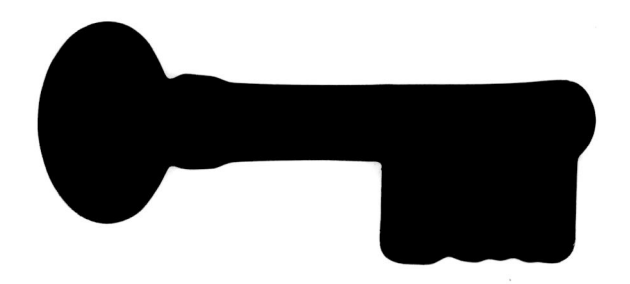

One particular friend who was always there for me was a very patient friend named, Troy. He devoted so much of his time to be by my side, listening and just sitting with me. He taught me, through his example, how I could be of service to another. Through, Troy, I learned that even if I had no material means to help I could still be of service. I'm not sure I could have gotten through this difficult period without his presence. His mentorship has shaped me to become the person I am today.

I remember that day when I recognized that hope had become my *modus operandi*. I started to go out just to get out of the house, but breathing in the fresh air changed my outlook. I decided to clean my surroundings, which purified me internally, as well. I attended to the dishes that had long been piling up in the sink. I scrubbed my bathroom, and I even took a long, relaxing shower. I was listening to music as a sort of therapeutic relief when it hit me: *hope* had become my new driver.

Sometimes, the depression would try to settle back in, but I

A Second Wind

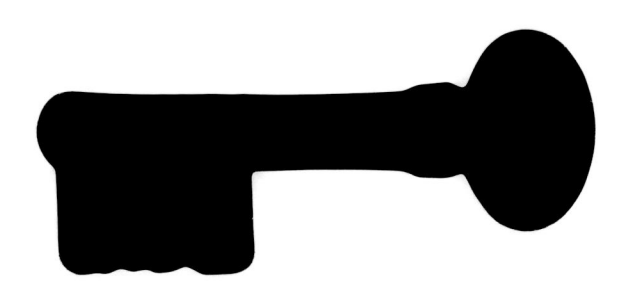

would always call someone. I would be sure to eat well, preparing food from scratch instead of nuking something still in plastic. When negative thoughts came into my head, I would tell myself, "I do not want to go back to that dark place again. I'm going to be doing something contrary to what my brain is telling me." So if my head said to "isolate," I would reach out and connect with someone. If it said, "Lie here and don't move," I would get up and go for a walk. It is important to recognize that my spirit had been lifted, but my situation had not yet changed. All of the reasons why I had fallen into my desolation were still there. At this moment, I simply had a little hope that I would not be like this forever, and that I had people in my life who were concerned. But despite this knowledge, I still felt powerless. Having the tiniest bit of hope did not magically make everything better. It did motivate me to get off the couch, however, and to get into action so that there would be a possibility of things slowly improving. It gave me the strength to look at the things I was afraid of and to take action. The phrase, "Faith without works is dead," springs to mind.

Jai Wurfbain

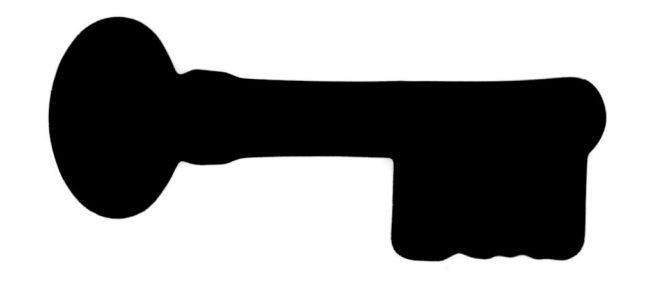

> **❝ Do not ask God to guide your footsteps, if you're not willing to move your feet. ❞**
> ~ Anonymous

I have long been mindful of a holistic lifestyle. This is just another way of saying "whole health." This is not to be confused with alternative medicine. While this can refer to alternative medicine practices, it also encompasses so much more. Common things such as sleeping well, exercise, and eating healthy are important practices that promote holistic well-being. For instance, my ability to act and react is dramatically impacted by my sleeping habits. When I truly understand this about myself, it is worth taking the time and effort to prepare myself for a good night's rest. I must be mindful when I don't get enough rest, as I will likely react with less mental strength when faced with stressful situations and less ability to avoid them. I had to be honest with myself and see how fatigue affected my thinking. As I mentioned earlier, I am very afraid of any kind of medication, so I was reluctant to take sleeping aids. Instead, I made sure to not drink coffee or other beverages containing caffeine after 3pm, to not eat a heavy meal too close to bedtime, and to be mindful not to over-stimulate my brain leading up to my sleep. In fact, toward the end of the day, I now take time to pray or meditate, which also allows me to reflect in a loving way on the past day. It's funny to look back at my old habit of always having the TV on in the background, thinking I couldn't fall asleep without it. Sometimes, our habits make us believe our lies and give attention to distractions. What I needed was a dark room, a proper diet, and vigorous exercise to help me sleep. But I opted for a box with lights instead.

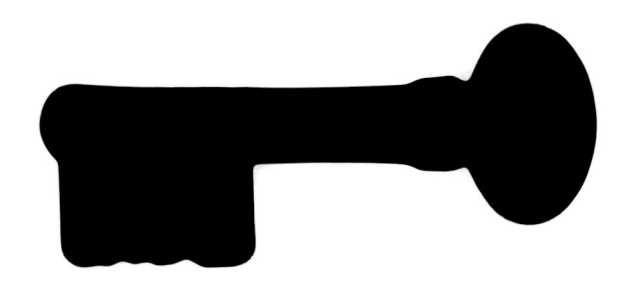

"Exercise till the mind feels delight in reposing from the fatigue."

~ Socrates

Jai Wurfbain

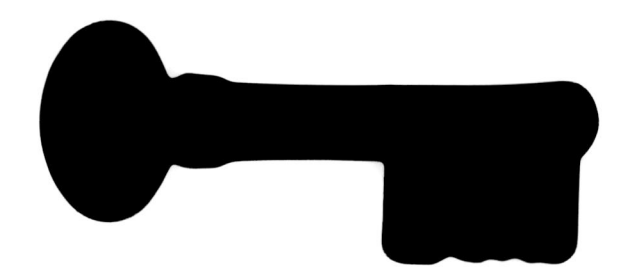

So, as soon as I was able to get out of bed, I knew I needed to go running or cycling, and that once I started, it would make me feel great again as it always had done before. From my own experience, I get better sleep, feel more energetic, and believe that I am a happier, more capable person ready to take on new challenges when I exercise. The stress of work had thoroughly impacted my regular working-out routine. In the past, I would work out daily for at least an hour. Now, I realized I had not done any exercise at all, in well over a year. I couldn't believe it had just added up like that, and that stress had kept me away from something I loved so immensely.

In my depression, each and every step seemed to weigh a thousand pounds. I simply didn't have the energy to even contemplate working out. My first run was seven miles in length, not something I would recommend to anyone, and I paid the price for it afterwards. However, I couldn't stop once I broke through my pain barrier about twenty minutes into my run. The endorphins kicked in, and they not only reduced my pain but gave me that "runner's high" that I craved so much. Exercise is a natural antidepressant. I would put on my headphones and just go. On my return, my

A Second Wind

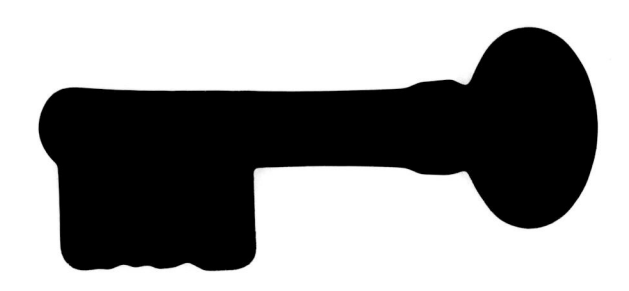

problems seemed just a little less difficult to face. And the shower afterwards may be one of the best feelings in the world. I felt as if my problems were being washed down the drain.

My diet has also always been important, and I have a passion for food. I love eating, I love cooking, and I love planning elaborate meals. My favorite TV shows are all about food. I even plan my vacations around food and possible cooking classes. What I enjoy the most, however, is the social aspect of food. It brings people together and gives us a vehicle for sharing intimate time. I get to combine seeing loved ones while pleasing the taste senses. Now, I invite people over to cook and eat together, and I practice my newly learned skill of opening-up to people at the same time. When I hit rock bottom, my appetite disappeared overnight and I couldn't eat anything. At one point I was forcing myself to eat, knowing that I really needed to eat something. During this period, I lost about twenty pounds. A lot of my low energy was compounded by my lack of calories—yet another example of me holding myself back. I also made a concerted effort to continue connecting with others. In particular, it became necessary for me to spend time with them on a social level that did not involve them helping me. It was important to start laughing again, to have humor back into my life.

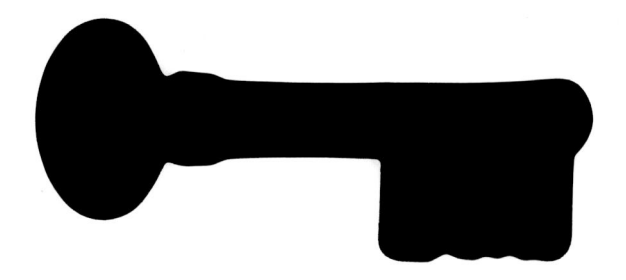

> **"I love people who make me laugh. I honestly think it's the thing I like most, to laugh. It cures a multitude of ills. It's probably the most important thing in a person."**
> ~ Audrey Hepburn

I find humor to be very uplifting and encouraging. Early in my recovery I had a conversation with a friend, where I laughed about something that she said to me. I can't remember what it was, but I suddenly came to the realization that I couldn't even remember the last time that I had laughed or seen humor in my life. That sudden injection of laughter in my life felt so good and lifted my spirits even more. I would make a point of watching movies or shows

A Second Wind

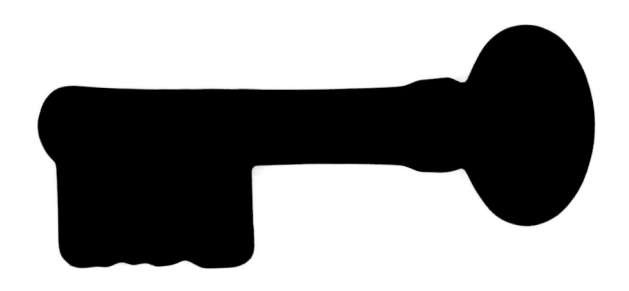

which were more likely to bring a smile to my face. I learned to avoid depressing dramas (though I loved the genre) because I just didn't want to risk having exasperating negative feelings again. Doing this with friends was very helpful. They would often center my attention on something funny that I may have missed because I was too "in my head" to honestly see what was happening. I tried to be lighthearted, and soon I began to find more hope where I once felt there was no hope to be had. I began to see things with an improved sense of clarity. That is what laughter does to my soul. It brought my mind in line with reality. Laughter strengthens me. I find that when I can have a few good laughs, my day is filled with so much more peace. When I have that peace, fear vanishes. Peaceful, happy hearts are what we all need to change the world, one heart at a time, and it begins with me! Today, I allow myself to laugh a little more and try to bring at least some joy into other people's lives. The Bible affirms the healing power of joy when it says, "A cheerful heart is good medicine, but a crushed spirit dries up the bones" (Prov. 17:22, NIV). This scriptural truth suggests that laughter holds as much healing power as does medicine.

Jai Wurfbain

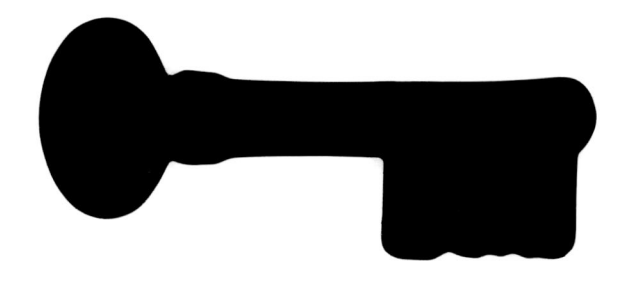

> **" A day without laughter is a day wasted. "**
> ~ Charlie Chaplin

Laughter releases powerful endorphins (which act much the same way as natural morphine) in the brain. Endorphins trigger a feeling of wellbeing. So, you see, a merry heart really does work like medicine! Laughter releases endorphins--body's own opiates. The endorphins induce a feeling of euphoria, excitement and satisfaction. The best kind of medicine is humor, which helps me discover new ways to experience myself. I can become quite critical of myself, and I now think it important to be able to laugh at myself, to be somewhat self-deprecating, in a humorous way. It sure beats crying. When I laugh, I shift my perceptions about life. This breaks up denser energies that clog our creative flow and allows us to see things from a fresh perspective. Humor and laughter benefit me in many ways. When I laugh with others, our connections deepen. I begin to feel more relaxed, and it is easier to be open-minded to a new perspective.

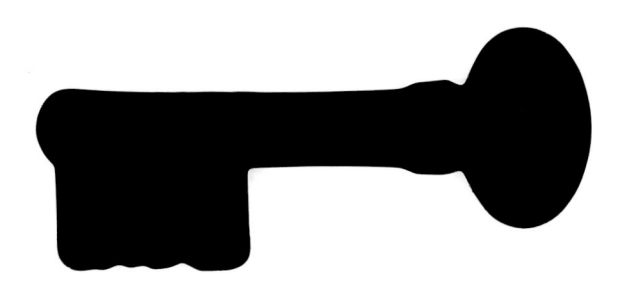

Laughter elevates energetic vibration. I cannot remain angry while laughing. Laughter opens the heart, increasing my capacity to love, forgive and to be compassionate. It lifts my emotional experience and positively influences my choices, and I feel healthier. In essence, laughter feels great!

It's important to consider that I have only listed five practical things that were essential to bring joy back into my life. They are food, exercise, sleep, connecting with others, and humor. I was careful in making sure that these remained as well balanced as I could manage. If these categories were taken care of, I was able to respond better, think more clearly, and be motivated to face life's challenges. These were not the only things that I worked on, however. I was open to suggestions from my friends, even though in the past, I would have treated recommendations with quiet contempt without even trying. For instance, I am personally not a very musically minded person, but listening to music helps me exercise longer and more intensely. I am very aware of the positive healing power that others enjoy through music and actively use it to improve their spiritual prosperity. In desiring to find more peace in my life, I try to put aside a little time to do what some of my friends have always done. When I actively pursue a feeling of calmness and serenity, it helps me to listen to some of my favorite music without doing anything else. This little practice became the stepping-stone to my meditation practice, something that I absolutely adhere to throughout each day. I did have to be careful about my choice in music, though, because sad music can amplify that mood.

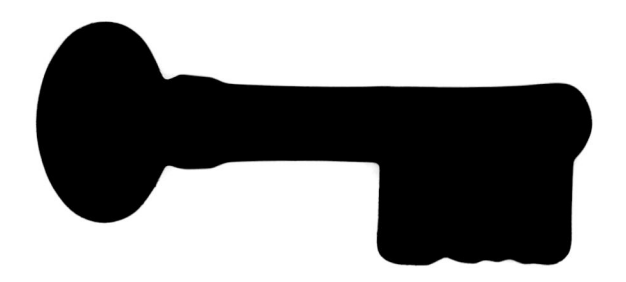

❖❖❖❖❖❖❖❖❖❖❖❖❖❖❖❖❖❖❖

> **❝*Music gives a soul to the universe, wings to the mind, flight to the imagination, and life to everything.*❞**
>
> ~ Plato

❖❖❖❖❖❖❖❖❖❖❖❖❖❖❖❖❖❖❖❖❖❖❖❖❖❖❖❖❖❖

Some of my friends also suggested that I find solace in nature.

A Second Wind

Taking walks was not something that I used to enjoy. Unless I was being "productive" or doing something that I knew there was some benefit from, because I felt like I was wasting my time. People had told me before that they would be in peace, but I was still under the impression that "I will have peace when everything works out" instead of, "*When I have peace everything works out.*" I thoroughly enjoyed activities such as scuba diving, skiing and running in nature, but I was always doing something instead of observing. This felt uncomfortable in the beginning, simply because I was not used to calm and serenity. But what a joy it is now to be able to calmly behold the beauty that exists all around us. Many years prior to this, someone had tried to teach me "walking meditation," but it never stuck until after I got sober. Walking meditation means becoming mindful of my experience in the moment, while walking. That guidance became meaningful to me and I finally learned the wisdom that was being passed onto me. I don't believe there is a limit to living holistically as a discipline. If it benefits my mind, body, and spirit, I should simply enjoy it. Today, I remain open to doing something a little different and give it a chance to work for me.

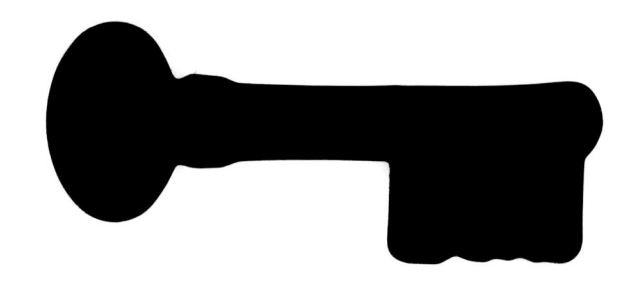

THE GOLDEN RULE

I want to mention the one practice that I credit as the absolute cure to my severe bout of depression. It can be credited for the quality of life that I enjoy today. Now, I certainly did not create some kind of miracle cure. It has always been there, and it has always been professed to work by professionals and spiritual leaders alike. Scriptures from all major religions mention it as the most meaningful act in life. It is referenced as the one purpose that brings personal fulfillment above anything else. There are several principles that all religions share. For instance, they all preach compassion, being kind to others, and selflessness. These principles combined, can be brought into one single principle that ALL religions in the world agree on–*service to others.* My life has been transformed by this golden rule! I've moved from feelings of low self-esteem, failure and anger to great levels of joy, gratitude, clarity and much more! How did I do it? By being of service to others—something anyone can do. I don't believe the kind of service matters, except that it cannot be done when you are expecting something in return.

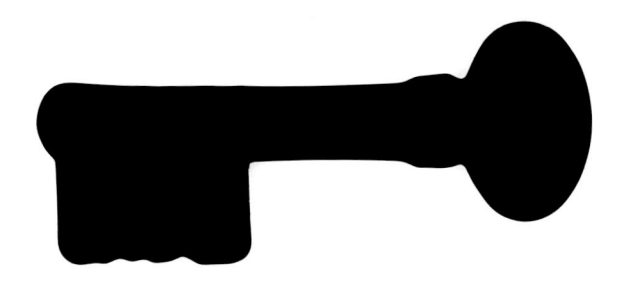

> ❝ *The best way to find yourself is to lose yourself in the service of others.* ❞
> ~ Mahatma Ghandi

Service to others, to me, means being unselfish. It means doing something for someone else without expecting any reward or gain. Service to others, to me, also means helping people when they cannot complete a task by themselves. There are many different ways to provide service to others, varying from helping someone carry their groceries to their car to serving your country in the military. By serving people, you are improving your character, and the character of those around you. People say that one act of kindness leads to another.

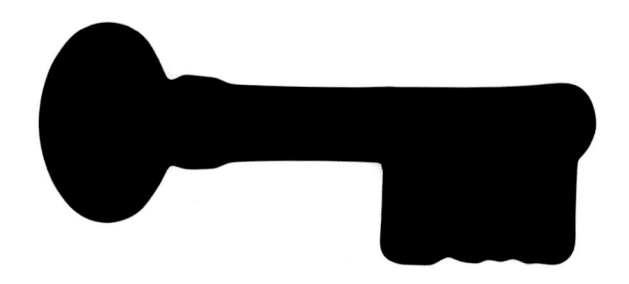

Soon after I lost my house, I became active in managing and running a sober living home. It was an old home in the center of town with single pane windows and very poor insulation, which made the cold Utah winters difficult at times. The house only had two bedrooms on the main floor, but the landlord had built another little studio above the garage, and there were several rooms in the basement that eventually got fitted out as bedrooms as well. It was by no means luxurious, but it sufficed very nicely for what I set out to do. All I needed it to do was to provide a safe, inexpensive living accommodation for those early in their recovery from alcohol and drugs. I charged very little to stay there, only $100 a week, which often made it quite the juggle to make ends meet. On more than one occasion, I did have to ask for outside donations to keep the bills paid, but we somehow always managed to keep the doors open for the next month. In the beginning, it was very difficult. I had little experience with the day-to-day difficulties of taking care of young adult males, who were, by nature of their disease, selfish and self-centered. They were often aggressive and seemingly always trying to hustle money, property, and female

The Golden Rule

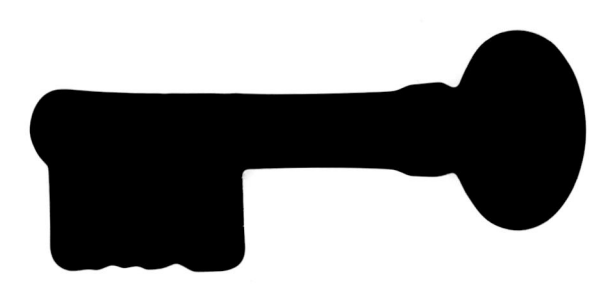

relationships. It certainly was never boring. I always thought this place would make a wonderful reality TV show. It was far removed from my old life, where I chased money, power, and prestige. At first, this humbling of self did not feel good. It still felt humiliating at times. But, ever so slowly, I began to see glimpses of reasons why I was where I was and doing what I was doing. I could see that the work I was doing was yielding some results in some long-term sobriety for some residents, and successes in the work gave me renewed energy at times when I was running low, myself.

One of my "guests" was a bear of a man that I had met in jail. His name is Kraig. He was about forty-eight when I first met him. He had been a career drug-addict since his teens. His drug of choice was meth, but he would snort, smoke or ingest just about anything he could get his hands on. There was a lot of physical violence on his rap sheet, and considering the size of this man, that was always a concern to any presiding judge. I'm fairly certain that there was some Viking blood in his ancestry—tall, blonde, and not afraid to hurt people.

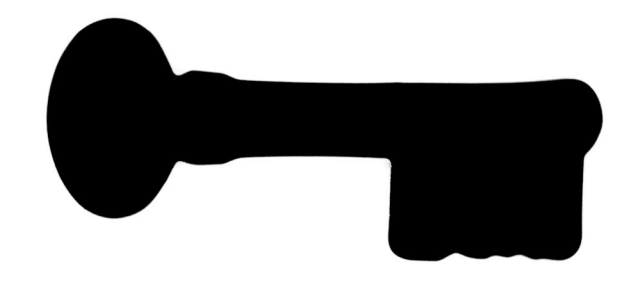

❖❖❖❖❖❖❖❖❖❖❖❖❖❖❖❖❖❖

"*Everybody can be great. . . because anybody can serve. You don't have to have a college degree to serve. You don't have to make your subject and verb agree to serve. You only need a heart full of grace. A soul generated by love.*"
~ Martin Luther King

❖❖❖❖❖❖❖❖❖❖❖❖❖❖❖❖❖❖❖❖❖❖❖❖❖❖❖

Kraig was awaiting trial that would almost certainly result in him being sent to prison for the third time in his life. We talked about the possibility of doing drug-court, but he was not hopeful that he would be able to participate, since he was too old, and his criminal history was way beyond the point where the court would consider him. However, I saw in him a willingness to change that I rarely saw in anyone. Most are willing to change on a temporary basis, but in order for long-term sobriety to have a chance, a much stronger form of willingness is required. It's the kind that can only be brought about by a level of suffering so deep and severe that a person becomes hopeful and willing to surrender all self-will in order to finally allow God to work in their lives without prejudice.

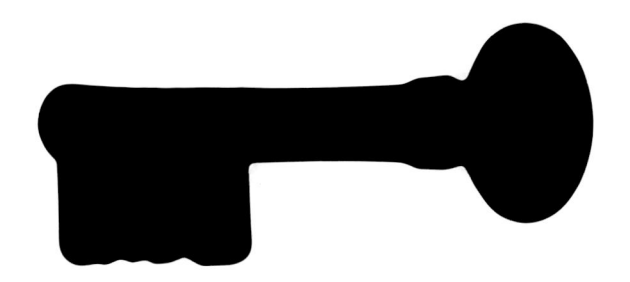

> *"Once you choose hope, anything's possible."*
> ~ Christopher Reeve

Kraig was willing. The drug court program accepted him, which was the lesser of two miracles. The more important one came first: Kraig surrendered. But he knew that drug court was never going to be easy. Drug court has a fantastic success rate for people that graduate the program—close to 75% never see another set of handcuffs again. But there is a very high dropout rate and it certainly isn't a walk in the park. Kraig had to attend a program five days a week and submit to "random" drug tests. There was no flexibility, even when this would clash with his work schedule. And there were program fees to be paid as well as fines and rent at my sober living home. Kraig was a union ironworker and was paid almost $40 an hour in his trade, but his work schedule clashed with his drug court program. Kraig and I agreed when we met that he *must* put his recovery first and everything else after. This also meant his finances. Thus, instead of working out of town for $40 an hour, he took flexible part-time work nearby that fit his recovery schedule, sometimes for less than $10 per hour. He went to multiple 12-step meetings a day and helped out at the house when needed. I lent him a bicycle, since he had lost his driver's license. The memory of watching him ride to and from work on this little bike still brings a smile to my face and puts a chuckle in my heart.

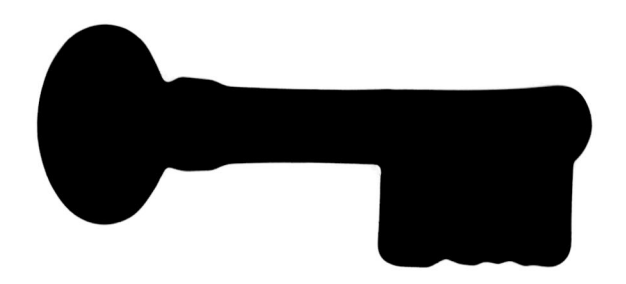

    The drug court program counselors loved Kraig, and he was asked to be an example to others new to the program. Kraig became my rock and my trusted confidant at my house. Whenever I lost hope due to someone's poor conduct or financial worries, Kraig was there to show me that it was worth it. Kraig also helped me get through emotionally tough days. He would tell others that

The Golden Rule

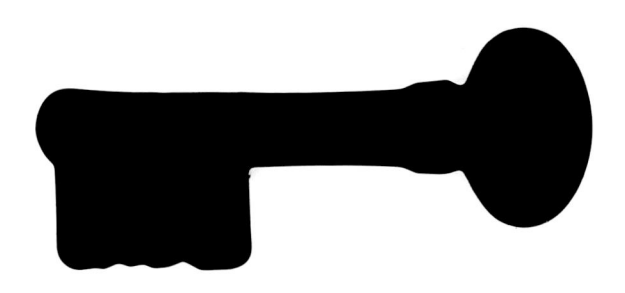

I helped him, whereas I know the truth was the other way around. He showed me the most magnificent change in a human being. I trust him implicitly, and he is one of the most honorable people I know. There was never an instance of violence and, even when deeply frustrated, he would not get angry or lose control. At the time of this writing, Kraig is coming up on four years of continued sobriety from any alcohol or drugs. He is back in the ironwork industry and was recently promoted to supervisor after working as a foreman for the last year. He has rebuilt his relationships with his children, which he never thought possible, and he is actively working at paying down the last portion of his fines and restitution that at one time amounted to more than $80,000.

He wasn't the only one to be successful, but his example gave me the strength every day to continue. He showed me God's magnificent work in motion once a person has decided to get out of the way. He also repaid his "debt" to me by being an example to his friends and colleagues, several of which moved in, seeking to change themselves for the better. He is a walking, talking miracle that I am honored to witness. God is good.

Doing this kind of service was not something that I ever thought

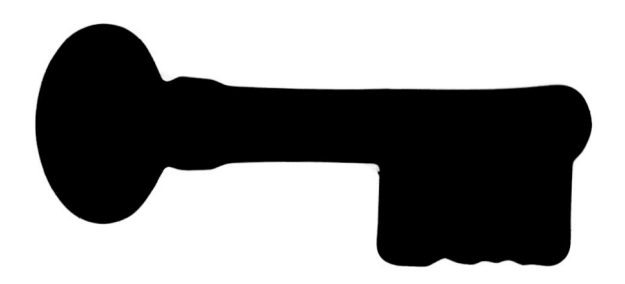

I would end up doing when I was little and dreaming of being successful. It was, however, the best thing I have ever done. Being of service got me "out of myself." Rather than focus on what I wasn't getting and how things weren't working out for me, I became active in being helpful in another person's life. Yes, at times it was tough, and there were times when self-pity reared its head. There were days where I felt very unappreciated and unloved! I wondered how people could think badly of me when all I was doing was trying to help. And I suffered when people would steal from me and talk bad about me in the community. However, it is a small price for the gratitude that I have learned to feel in being of service.

My humility is dependent on what I learned by being of service. I know today that humility is the basis of the strength and the power that allows me to do more than I'm capable of by myself. No longer do I live a life dominated by selfish and greedy motivations. Through my service, I started to see aspects of my life, past and present with a much greater sense of understanding and gratitude. Holding gratitude in our hearts does amazing things, the most profound of all being that it multiplies. Gratitude embodies everything that is love. In gratitude, I feel connected with everything and everyone. There is nothing out of place and nothing that can be said to me that will take away that peace and serenity that exists in my heart. In gratitude, fear is absent and the words "more," "but," and "if," have been banished from my language. I am temporarily brandishing a shield that is impervious to negativity. The universe and everything in it is perfect. In many ways, I see it as a spiritual awakening every time I reach this place of wellbeing.

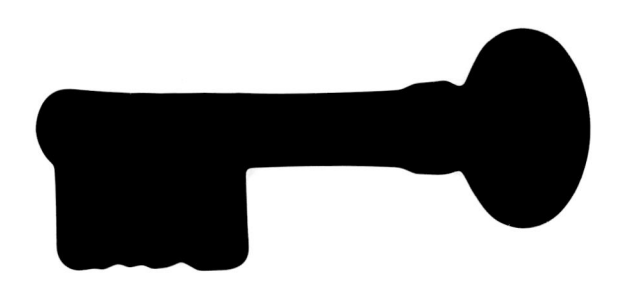

I've never had a burning bush moment, but when I am in genuine gratitude, it feels as if the whole world is on fire. Service is my keystone to gratitude. I can actually feel the resonance with the phrase "the gift of service." How true! My hope is that you will go out and serve and, like me, find that it might unlock your own inner sense of gratitude.

If you try something and don't find it rewarding, try something else. But use every service experience to learn or affirm something. Going into my project, I was not expecting my world to change, but it did. And so can yours.

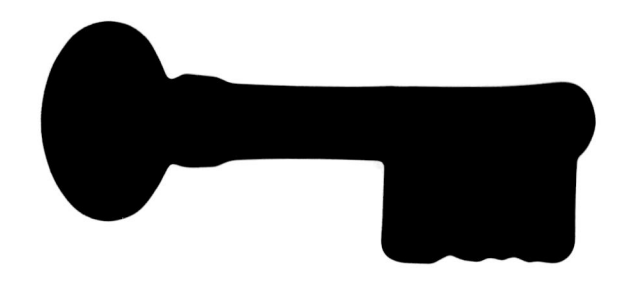

EPILOGUE

My life today is by no means perfect, which is to say that not everything works out just as I want. But then again, the biggest realization I came to is that it doesn't have to. Everything works out beautifully without a need for me to stick my dirty little digits into other people's pies. I heard someone share once, "If I had gotten what I wanted, I would have short-changed myself." I recognize that phrase to be true for me as well. I keep it close to my heart, since I need regular reminders that I need to let go of expectations. There isn't a problem in planning and having goals, but my life has never been dependent on the outcome of my choosing. If someone had told me twenty years ago what I would be doing today, or that I would have the values that I possess now, I would have laughed at, and most likely, ridiculed him or her.

I will forever be grateful for my material losses. Mostly, because I will no longer place power and money as the most valu-

Epilogue

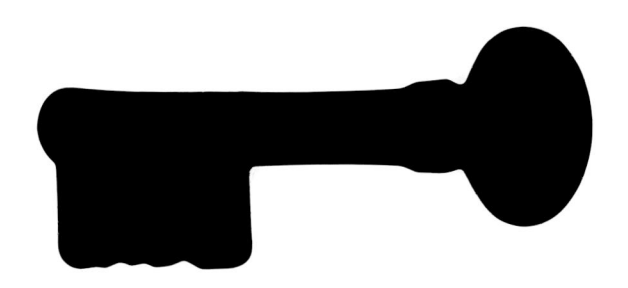

able commodities in my life. I have many goals that I would like to achieve and I will never stop working towards them. Living my amends to those that I have harmed is a lifelong exercise. I lack in seeing my children as often as I should. I have financial concerns that need to be addressed. I have relationships that need to be nurtured—all these things and more. Every one of these, need to be worked on but I can only do these things properly when I maintain a fit spiritual condition. Which means never forgetting my suffering, being present in the moment, recognizing that tomorrow isn't guaranteed and remembering to live purposefully and gently. Ensuring that my actions don't cause unnecessary harm to others or myself.

Sure, there are moments of regret when I think of all that I could still have if I had made better choices. But I wasn't ready then to accept any changes. I needed to go through every ounce of suffering to become open-minded and willing to embrace the necessary changes that have granted me a new lease on life. The lessons that I learned and took from head to heart will yield me a lifelong ability to live gratefully in God's world. And finally, I get to write my last words on why it is imperative that we keep

Jai Wurfbain

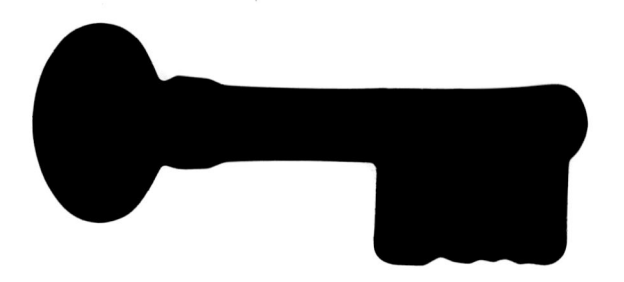

"hope" close in our hearts. They are simply this: "without hope, we are hopeless, and to be hopeless is to die spiritually."

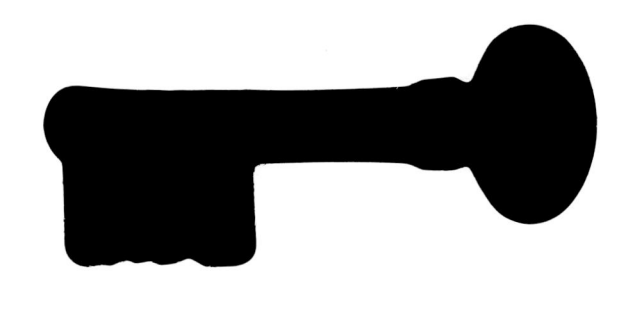

Epilogue

❖❖❖❖❖❖❖❖❖❖❖❖❖❖❖❖❖~

"When I was a young man, I wanted to change the world. I found it was difficult to change the world, so I tried to change my nation. When I learned that I couldn't change the nation, I began to focus on my town. I couldn't change the town and as an older man, I tried to change my family. Now, as an old man, I realize the only thing I can change is myself, and suddenly I realize that if long ago I had changed myself, I could have made an impact on my family. My family and I could have made an impact on our town. Their impact could have changed the nation and I could indeed have changed the world."

- Unknown Monk (1100AD)

❖❖❖❖❖❖❖❖❖❖❖❖❖❖❖❖❖❖❖

Kickstarter sponsorship.

As a struggling artist (I've always wanted to call myself that), I was unable to fund this project entirely by myself. It's taken me almost 12 months start to finish, and during this time, I've relied on the generosity of friends and family to give me a safe harbor and fill my belly. Don't feel too sorry for me, since I've never been short on anything. I feel well provided for, and I know who to credit for that.

One of my Kickstarter rewards were for people pledging a large amount to make this endeavor happen.

A special thank you to those that "sponsored" this dream;

Dave & Martha Read, Tom Quick, John Horne, Kay Upchurch, Noi Namman, Debbie Smart, Sallie Dawson, Christine Stroobosscher, Tom Sayer, Gloria Smart, Donna Dasinger and Tom Pfahler

Thank you !!!

Disclaimer

WARNING

Keep out of reach of children or adults that still think or act like children. For your safety and that of others.

The key inside of this book MUST NOT be ingested, licked, get stuck in orifices or anything that a sensible person would NOT think of doing. The same goes for the glue. Fugitive glue (also known as booger glue) must be carefully removed and disposed of for reasons mentioned above.

To ignore this warning will not only cause physical harm, it may cause for others to laugh heartily at you which might hurt your feelings. We cannot be liable for emotional distress that this causes either.

Please… Just don't!

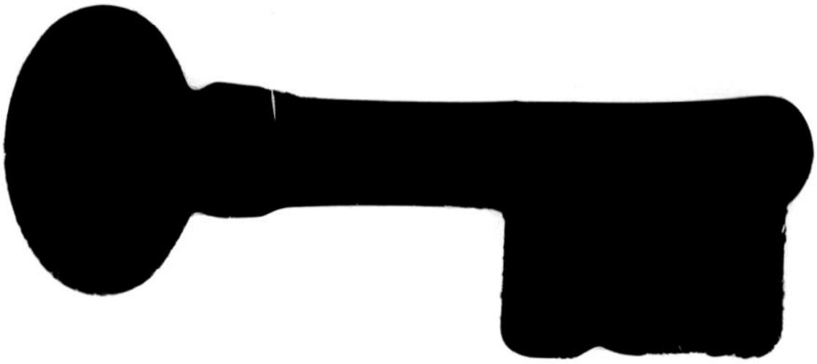